Jewish Lunacy

Dave,

Hineni. Here I am.

God bless always!

Eric o Tygrrrr Express

Jewish Lunacy

6000 Years of Tradition, Pride, and Stories as Told by Someone Who Missed the First 5,960 Years

eric aka the TYGRRRR EXPRESS

JEWISH LUNACY
6000 YEARS OF TRADITION, PRIDE, AND STORIES AS TOLD BY SOMEONE WHO MISSED THE FIRST 5,960 YEARS

Copyright © 2015 eric aka the Tygrrrr Express.

All rights reserved. No part of this book may be used or reproduced by any means, graphic, electronic, or mechanical, including photocopying, recording, taping or by any information storage retrieval system without the written permission of the author except in the case of brief quotations embodied in critical articles and reviews.

iUniverse books may be ordered through booksellers or by contacting:

iUniverse
1663 Liberty Drive
Bloomington, IN 47403
www.iuniverse.com
1-800-Authors (1-800-288-4677)

Because of the dynamic nature of the Internet, any web addresses or links contained in this book may have changed since publication and may no longer be valid. The views expressed in this work are solely those of the author and do not necessarily reflect the views of the publisher, and the publisher hereby disclaims any responsibility for them.

Any people depicted in stock imagery provided by Thinkstock are models, and such images are being used for illustrative purposes only.
Certain stock imagery © Thinkstock.

ISBN: 978-1-4917-6021-5 (sc)
ISBN: 978-1-4917-6022-2 (hc)
ISBN: 978-1-4917-6020-8 (e)

Library of Congress Control Number: 2015903333

Print information available on the last page.

iUniverse rev. date: 10/13/2015

Eric is the proud Hebrew alpha male behind *The Tygrrrr Express*, the 2007 Bloggers Choice Award for Most Passionate Fan Base.

He is also the author of the books *Ideological Bigotry, Ideological Violence, Ideological Idiocy* and *Ideological Lunacy*.

The Tygrrrr Express has been published in the *Washington Times, Jewish Journal, RealClearPolitics Online, Commentary Magazine Online*, and many other publications.

A sought after public speaker, he has addressed many college campuses, women's groups, Jewish and non-Jewish political groups, and synagogues. He has spoken in many Jewish delis, but mainly just to order his food.

A radio host on and off since 1992, his radio beginning was a sophomoric hard rock music program. Maturation eventually settled in (some disagree), and serious radio interviews with top politicos and other notables ensued. On the flip side of the microphone, he has been a radio guest of many top programs.

At his core, he is a proud Jew, son and grandson of Holocaust survivors, and mitzvah boy who met the Lubavitcher Rebbe twice.

In 1990 he held the top score for video football at the local arcade, which has nothing to do with Judaism and impresses nobody. One week after he left for college, a power failure at the arcade erased this part of his legacy forever. For this and other reasons, books on Jewish history are not expected to contain his achievement.

About: *The Tygrrrr Express* is me. I was born in Brooklyn, raised on Long Island, and am currently living in Los Angeles. A long-time stockbrokerage and oil professional, Wall Street is forever in my blood. In 2009 I left the financial world and am now on the speaking circuit full-time.

I like Judaism, politics, the National Football League, 1980s hard rock music, the stock market, and red meat. At some point I will marry a lovely Jewish brunette. This ceremony has to happen in short order because my parents are members of the National Rifle Association. They are fully prepared to shoot me if they are not given Jewish grandchildren soon. I offered to pick up random kids from the local grocery store. My parents made it clear their grandchildren must enter the world by me the traditional way.

eric aka *The Tygrrrr Express*

To my four grandparents: Although you are gone, you are with me every day. When I do right, it is because I know you are watching me. Yes grandpa, I got a haircut. It was awhile back. I know, I promise I'll get another one at some point.

Some of you will point out that Judaism has only been around for 5,775 years. Those who know me know that I only missed the first 5,733 years. Let it go. Abraham lived for 175 years. If any of you are alive in 225 years, pick up this book and see that the numbers I quote on the front cover are accurate.

Contents

Chapter 0: Unlike a Siddur, this foreword is read forward xiii

Chapter 1: Youthful Lunacy: The one religion that tolerates me. 1

Chapter 2: College Lunacy: My failure to become the world's greatest theologian 8

Chapter 3: Grandparent Lunacy: No Grandpa, I'm not married 20

Chapter 4: Grandparent Lunacy Part II: Yes Grandpa, I got another haircut 26

Chapter 5: Parental Lunacy: The curse of having normal parents 36

Chapter 6: Palestinian Lunacy: A rich history spanning almost 45 years 46

Chapter 7: Secular Lunacy: Orthodox Jews get virtually everything right 55

Chapter 8: Sexual Lunacy: How I became Shomer Negiah 60

Chapter 9: Sports Lunacy: My career as a Jewish football player 65

Chapter 10: Dancing Lunacy: Nobody parties like a sharp dressed Chabad Rabbi 76

Chapter 11: Philosophical Lunacy: When is a speech not a speech? 83

Chapter 12: Internal Jewish Lunacy: Too Jewish vs. not Jewish enough 92

Chapter 13: Vocational Lunacy: More stockbrokers, fewer teachers and social workers 100

Chapter 14: Political Lunacy: The Torah is non-partisan 106

Chapter 15: Pacifist Lunacy: Hanukkah, the Six-Day War and the IDF 110

Chapter 16: Conspiracy Lunacy: The Zionist Crusader Alliance for World Domination 115

Chapter 17: Religious Lunacy: Not everyone is Jewish 123

Chapter 18: Chai, how are you doing? Next Generation Lunacy 132

Chapter 0: Unlike a Siddur, this foreword is read forward

My first three books *Ideological Bigotry*, *Ideological Violence* and *Ideological Idiocy* are all political. Those books became part of a political book and speaking tour that took me to all fifty states. My fourth book *Ideological Lunacy* is also political. While the tour has been financially rewarding, something was missing. Virtually all of my audiences have been non-Jewish. A desire to spend more time speaking to my own people required offering words that most Jews can appreciate. Politics is divisive. Some Jews will never shake my hand because of political differences. Telling the story of 6,000 years of Jewish history is something Orthodox, Conservative, Reform and Reconstructionist Jews can appreciate.

The problem with covering all 6,000 years of Jewish history is that I missed most of it. I also missed the classes where we studied the people who studied the people who studied the people who were there at the beginning. It would be the height of arrogance to think I could compete with Rashi and RaMBaM in retelling what must be told. Starting a sentence with tales of the Lubavitcher Rebbe or the Baal Shem Tov would please nobody. Secular Jews would be bored. Religious Jews would be correcting every word I said. Apparently Adam Sandler did not play the Zohar.[1]

What I am qualified to do is discuss the four decades of Judaism I witnessed. This eliminates countries I have never visited and people I have never met. My sphere of influence contains my family, friends and readers when they actually listen to me.

My family is so secretive and anonymous that even they are not sure who they are. They have so many questions about me that they cannot begin to ask about you. I would ask about you but I have a ton of questions about me as well.

Telling a few lighthearted anecdotes about my family and friends may not seem as important as what the sages teach us, but my stories are still Jewish history. I am a part of Jewish history. If you are Jewish, then you are as well. Every Jew extends Jewish history.

Although critics have described much of my thinking as backward, this book is not holy enough to be read backward like a Siddur. Although my Jewish history occurs at the end, this book is best read from the beginning.

This may be the least important Jewish book written in the next 6,000 years, but even being the tiniest Hebrew slice of a 12,000-year pie would be an honor. As I tell Jewish brunettes on my potential wife list, it is easy to be this handsome when I belong to a religion this beautiful.

Enjoy learning about 6,000 years of Jewish history with the first 5,960 years left out.

Welcome to Jewish Lunacy.

Chapter 1: Youthful Lunacy: The one religion that tolerates me

My Jewish faith is a source of pride, but also a reason for relief. Judaism does not excommunicate people. Judaism is like the Mafia. Unless one has pure bloodlines, getting into the family is difficult. Those born into the family have a lifetime connection. Even those who convert away from Judaism never truly leave.

My Jewish history began in 5733, known to the Christians as 1972. From the beginning, my confusion with Judaism was matched only by Judaism's puzzlement over me.

Born in the Holy Land

I was born in the Holy Land. That's right, Brooklyn, New York. Brooklyn is the greatest city in the world. People of all stripes live there in peace. Think of Brooklyn as Israel except with more pizza and less hummus. Questioning the judgment of Hashem who created everything may be brazen, but hummus is really an unnecessary creation.

As for where in Brooklyn I was born, I have no idea. The expected "What do you mean you have no idea where you were born?" response just leads me to repeat that I have no idea. I could call my parents right now and ask them. They know. I just never bothered to ask.

This issue only came up due to an accidental conversation with a random stranger outside a Jewish deli in South Florida. I held a door open for an elderly man (nice Jewish boys respect their elders) and he noticed my New York accent. He asked where I was from and I told him Brooklyn. Since virtually every Jew is from Brooklyn, he pointed out that my answer did not narrow down anything. I gave him the standard answer I have been giving my whole life, telling him, "I am a Coney Island Kid, Neptune (Avenue) and West Fifth (Street)." My mother interrupted and said, "Eric, don't tell people that. It's not true. You were born on Avenue (insert some letter here. I forgot)."

I always believed I was born near Coney Island. My four grandparents lived in the same building on Neptune and West Fifth for decades. The rest of my dad's side of the family lived across the street from them. The rest of my mom's side of the family lived a few minutes away. That is what I know.

Comedian Steven Wright once said, "I reminisce with people I don't know. It takes longer."[2] My reminiscing with strangers takes place at Neptune and West Fifth. Down the block from where my grandparents lived is the Key Foods. Across the street is the park. The elderly Jews sitting in both places do not know my first name, but they revered my grandparents.

My grandparents are gone, but their legacy is the best gift they could have ever given me. While I probably lived a few blocks away from what I tell people, my story is true in the sense of what I know. My parents will read this and correct the record. Until then, I am a Coney Island kid not too far from Sheepshead Bay.

Telling a story of 6,000 years of Jewish history is tough when a man does not even know his own birthplace. Then again, I only lived in Brooklyn for eight or nine months. After that my family moved to Long Island. I lived there for eighteen years. For those who have never been to Long Island, save your money. There is no reason to go whatsoever. From the home my parents raised me in, the key time travel was twenty minutes. If you went twenty minutes in any direction, there was something. We were twenty minutes from several things that people would consider civilization.

There were few Jews in this area. While my family was not Orthodox, the rabbis who reached out were. Rabbi Mordecai Golshevsky helped prepare me for my Bar Mitzvah. The rest of my main teachers were Chabad rabbis. While Rabbi Golshevsky stayed in the same town, the other Chabad rabbis moved all over the country. Teaching me did not inspire them to greatness, nor did it cause them to leave my town in frustration. Rabbi Leibel Baumgarten now spreads Chasidim to the stars in the Hamptons. Rabbi Yudul Lazar is in Lancaster, a town 90 minutes North of Los Angeles. Rabbi Yisroel Goldstein, son of the late famous Uncle Yossi, is in Poway in San Diego County. Back then they were all new rabbis in my small neighborhood searching out every Jew and helping pass down 6,000 years of traditions.

One reason I was destined to be a Jew is that Judaism is perhaps the only religion that could accept me and tolerate my antics. Judaism teaches us to question things. I have a deep respect for Christianity, but Christianity seems to tell children to just shut up and not ask questions. It was no wonder my proud Jewish father respected Christians so much. He would have made a great Pope. There was no dissent.

Apparently it is not acceptable for children to ask priests harmless questions about non-controversial issues such as abortion. Is it ok for a woman to have an abortion if the child would grow up to have two abortions? Can a temporary minus one be allowed to prevent a future minus two, rendering the original minus one a net plus one? Not all Catholic priests are experts in advanced mathematics, and not all of them answer philosophical questions with polite language. Who knew the priestly handbook allowed for responses starting with "Get the" and ending with "out of here!"

At least clergy people did not have to deal with me on a daily basis. My parents are retired schoolteachers, which meant my grades were a topic of discussion because they said so. I earned A's in reading, math, spelling and English and B's in social studies and science. Handwriting was a C grade. Despite my protesting that handwriting was not a subject, my parents insisted that it was.

Nowadays many children do not even have to learn cursive writing. Whether this is good or bad for society is irrelevant. This is about me. On the one hand I think that every child should be forced to suffer through composing handwritten thank-you notes like I did after my Bar Mitzvah. Then again, not one single lawyer will help me sue my third grade teacher for the carpal tunnel syndrome I probably developed writing all those words illegibly.

My third grade teacher told me that she would base my entire quarter handwriting grade on the last day of the period. If I could submit B handwriting for one day, she would give me the B. When my report card was handed to me later that day, all she could muster was a C+. There was only one thing for an honest boy from a good Jewish family to do. I took a pencil and clumsily changed the handwriting grade to a B+.

Later that night, I sat upstairs in my room as my parents prepared to give me a lecture about lying. They had no idea what they were in for. They called me downstairs, and my father calmly spoke.

"Son, I need to ask you something important. Did you change the handwriting grade on your report card?"

I looked at my parents and exclaimed, "Of course I did." This may have been the only time these two bright educators were completely befuddled. My dad explained that teachers and students are called that for a reason. I got my parents to admit that teachers were not perfect, and that everybody makes mistakes. The phrase "Again, you don't get to decide this" was repeated many times. My parents knew they had an honest child, but would probably have preferred to give a simple lecture about lying rather than the "You're not Hashem" lecture that took them several hours. That may have been the night my dad's hair turned gray. Their message did sink in, although it took almost thirty years after they had hoped.

If ever there was a case for religious education, it is the failed experiment known as public schools. Public schools are where kids go to die. Being a Jew among non-Jewish kids at a non-Jewish school is about as joyful as being a Jew in Saudi Arabia.

At age five the rocket scientists my local public school hired to instruct me in my formative years nearly slowed my development permanently. The administrators called my parents in and recommended that I be put in remedial special education classes. When my father asked what subject was troubling me, he was aghast at hearing the problem was math. My incredulous father insisted that I was a math genius and that there had to be a mistake.

My father began rattling off math questions that I correctly answered with rapid-fire precision.

The stunned secular teachers, in what would be a pattern that continued for much of my existence, had no answers. When told I scored only twenty-five percent, my father asked if these incredibly bright people looked at my test. When the academic bureaucrats explained that it was a Scantron computer printout they had not examined, he asked them if perhaps they should read the thing. Once they deigned to actually look at my test, they quickly discovered that my problem was not math.

The first twenty-five questions on the front of the paper were all answered correctly. Had I turned the page I would have seen an additional fifty questions in the middle and twenty-five more questions on the back. Leaving the last seventy-five questions blank was not the best way to ace this test.

My father asked me why I did not turn the page. I showed him the bottom of the front page where it said, "Stop. Do not continue until you are told to do so." Most of my academic life would see me get into trouble for defying instructions. The one time I did what I was told nearly caused the intellectual equivalent of Chernobyl.

My exasperated dad offered to have me take a flat test where all four pages would be spread out on the floor. The academic masterminds declared this unnecessary. One of them even pointed out that the twenty-five questions I did answer were all correct. With a score of one hundred percent that was expected to remain that way, one teacher suggested to my parents that I be put in the gifted and talented program for the exceptionally bright children.

At this point my father could no longer tolerate the stupidity of his fellow professionals. He barked that, "The kid does not know to turn the page. He's not a genius. He's not special ed. Just put him with the regular kids and leave him alone!"

Not every teacher in a Jewish day school is spectacular. Not every public schoolteacher is an oaf. The occasional private school does fail and the occasional public school bucks the odds and succeeds. After eliminating the extremes, a religious education still provides a better education than most public schools. Yeshiva students who spend all day learning Torah are often too tired intellectually and physically to get into fistfights over articles of clothing they should not be wearing anyway. Yeshivas are like public schools except for the standards. Yeshivas have them.

Outside of public school, my life was reasonably joyful. Attending Gan Yisroel sleep-away camp and National Conference of Synagogue Youth (NCSY) weekend Shabbatons enriched my Jewish faith. Like many Jewish children, I was proud to be one of Uncle Moishy's Mitzvah Men.

A true highlight of my Jewish life was encountering the Lubavitcher Rebbe Menachem Schneerson. The Rebbe spent his entire life teaching Jews that every mitzvah brings us closer to Moshiach, the beauty of world peace. As the head of the Chasidic sect of Judaism known as Chabad, the Rebbe remains every bit as influential in passing as he did while alive.

Far too many non-Orthodox Jews see Chasidic Jews as zealots. This is disturbing from a survival standpoint and an intelligence standpoint. There are too few Jews alive for us to cannibalize each other into warring sects. Sanity would dictate that dancing while holding a Torah and yelling, "We want Moshiach now!" is not the same thing as flying airplanes into towers. Most people not affiliated with terrorism cells, *CNN* or college universities grasp this simple concept.

My first encounter with the Rebbe came when I was eight years old. Farbrengens (joyous gatherings) and Hakofeses are filled with Jews eating, drinking, dancing and praying. The Rebbe was sitting in his chair at 770 in Crown Heights, Brooklyn, as thousands of Jews celebrated inside and outside the sanctuary. Being an incredibly small child physically allowed me to slip through the tiniest crevices. This allowed me to get so close to the Rebbe that I was sitting behind him playing with his holy tzitzis garments.

One of the elders was looking at me the way Pharaoh looked at a young Moses when Moses took Pharaoh's crown and placed it on his own head. The visual scolding was unnecessary. My hands were clean. I washed them. I even did so using the ritual Jewish cup followed by the appropriate hand-washing blessings.

Five years later came the reckoning. My mother and I were outside 770 when we saw the Rebbe greeting children. As was his custom, he would hand each child a dollar that they would then give to charity or use for some other mitzvah. Again, this was the leader of a scary cultish religious sect. Teaching children to give to charity and help the poor are dangerous ideas that if not stopped could lead to outbreaks of peace, love and happiness.

When the Rebbe gave me a dollar, he had several messages for me. He smiled and said something in Yiddish that translated into, "You shouldn't play with the rabbi's strings."

How does an elderly man with less than perfect vision remember a child from one encounter five years earlier? He then told me that I should try to get along better with my sibling.

He ended things on a positive note by telling me that my Bar Mitzvah went well.

As I stood there in shock, my mother looked at me and insisted that she did not tell the Rebbe a thing.

I knew from that moment on that I had met a very special man. I vowed that I would dedicate my life to learning his teachings. That vow would not be kept. I suspect if I had followed his path, the man I am and the man I could be would have already converged. When told it is never too late, my response is a shrug of the shoulders.

This has been the paradox of my Jewish history. Despite being surrounded by Orthodox Judaism, I went four decades without being Orthodox. On one side of me were secular Jews who had no interest in living a Jewish life. On the other side were Jews who obeyed all of the laws and took the 613 mitzvahs seriously. I remained mired in the middle, a Jew who deeply respected and believed in the religious traditions but did not obey them. As I got older, this struggle would only intensify, especially when I found out why I did not live the Jewish life I admired.

Chapter 2: College Lunacy: My failure to become the world's greatest theologian

After eighteen years in New York, it was time to move to Los Angeles. My college years were spent at the University of Judaism, now American Jewish University. Our class valedictorian gave one of the greatest commencement speeches in the history of graduation ceremonies. He calmly intoned that he arrived at the UJ an agnostic and was leaving a full-blown atheist. Many of us exchanged high-fives in the back, proud to stick it to the institution.

I am older now. I now know that I could have been more diplomatic about certain situations. On other issues, I grow more right as time goes by. Attending the UJ pushed me far away from Judaism. Leaving the UJ brought me back to it. In a perverse way, the UJ played an important role in my Jewish history.

Anarchy in the UJ

I never wanted to attend college. My goal of making it as a stockbroker on Wall Street does not even require a high school diploma. My father and I reached an understanding during my senior year in high school. I would attend college, and in return he would not beat the daylights out of me. He came up to my room one Sunday and turned off the television during my beloved football game. The television was not going back on until I filled out some college applications.

When he came back upstairs he saw the pile of schools I was interested in and the schools I had decided to avoid. My rejection pile included Harvard, Yale, and many other good schools. After eighteen years in New York, I never wanted to experience cold weather ever again. I only applied to colleges in Los Angeles and Florida.

I found this slick black brochure from the University of Judaism in Los Angeles. The weather was nice and I could go see some Raiders games. Filling out the application was less painful than the possibility of missing the end of the football game. I was accepted to begin my four years of wasting time before I could take the Series 7 stockbroker's exam.

My freshman year in college was one of the worst years I ever had. Angelenos at my school seemed to think that every New Yorker knew John Gotti and carried a gun. If I raised my voice and reached in my pocket for a pen or a comb, the pampered West Coast students thought I was about to shoot everybody. This was several years before those tragic situations actually started happening.

My first semester saw me come down with galloping pneumonia, the same disease that took the life of *Muppets* creator Jim Henson. After being hooked up to some hospital object that resembled a telephone pole, my close friend Eric did something I desperately needed. With doctors warning me to watch the food I ate, Eric picked me up from the hospital and took me to Sizzler. When I die, I want my last meal to be a steak.

On top of illness, a fellow student declared me public enemy number one because I went out for pizza with a girl he had a crush on. The situation was very romantic. The girl told me she was going for pizza and I asked if she would bring me back some. She told me not to be lazy, and that if I wanted some I could go with her to get it myself. It may seem silly for this to lead to conflict, but the Greeks and Trojans were ready to fight to the death over

Helen. Why should Jewish boys be any different just because the pizza is kosher?

This guy and I were both hotheads with serious chips on our respective shoulders. While he definitely started it, I was no stranger to pouring gasoline on a fire. I had a mouth, and was not shy about using it. He lost his scholarship and had to attend classes at a community college. He returned to the UJ even angrier. I thought he was just a meathead, a dumb jock. In retrospect, he was dealing with some emotional pain that he did not create and no person should have to deal with. Had I offered an outstretched hand, a mild conflict could have possibly stayed mild. Maybe it would have blown up anyway. Maybe he would have seen kindness as weakness. Jewish law declares a boy a man at age thirteen. American law does so at eighteen and in some cases twenty-one. Real manhood takes much longer than that. We were boys.

I was laughing with some friends in the classroom before class started. When somebody asked what was going on, Community College Boy out of nowhere said, "Eric's just talking (stuff) again." Not willing to be humiliated in front of my friends by an inferior intellect, I coolly responded, "You don't belong here. Go back to Pierce." CCB leapt out of his chair and came at me physically. I defended myself as other students pulled us apart just as the professor was walking in.

The professor was my first Dean of Students, a rabbi who taught ancient Jewish civilization. Despite more than one student telling him what really happened, he declared the incident a fight and admonished both CCB and me. CCB got probation and I received a tongue-lashing.

I felt the professor was taking the easy way out. He was more interested in a fake temporary calm than in sorting out the facts. He felt I was barbaric. This conflict dynamic ran deeper than one professor trying to discipline two warring students. The heart of public education and Judaism itself wrestles with an important issue.

When is it acceptable to hit back?

In public schools, if one kid starts a fight and the other kid retaliates, both kids are punished. To me, justice requires assigning culpability. Forced equality should never occur when behavior is unequal. There is no cycle of violence when one guy is trying to take another guy's head off and the other guy just wants to be left alone. When the aggressor and the victim are treated equally, the aggressor just becomes more aggressive. This is why bullies thrive

Jewish Lunacy

in public schools. Getting suspended is not a punishment for people who have no desire to attend school in the first place.

Israel faces this struggle every day. Hawks want Israel to hit back hard against her Arab enemies. Doves hold out the notion that an outstretched hand works better than a clenched fist.

The Dean had a fundamentally different view of the world than I did. He still does. He frequently lectures about the painful choices Israel needs to make peace. I prefer a more effective approach. Go Roman or go home.

While this Dean left after my freshman year, his successor shared his view of the world. She suffered from Harvard syndrome, the need to mention in every third sentence to anyone within earshot that she went to Harvard. Then again, nobody forced me to skip applying to a first-rate institution just because of cold weather.

She called me into her office to introduce herself. This woman who had never met me before began by lecturing me about fighting. She also told me that theft was wrong. This was a surprise to hear since I had never stolen anything in my life. She explained that people who get into fights also engage in other anti-social behavior such as theft. They teach many math classes at Harvard, but apparently logic is not one of them.

My nickname for this bureaucrat with gigantic shoulder pads was Lech Walesa. She was a solidarity crusher. I told people she was a third round NFL draft pick out of Clemson who would have gone pro if not for a bum knee. She was totally wrong about me, but I never bothered to get to know her either.

Like many Jewish academics, she sadly went on to become a Palestinian sympathizer openly critical of Israel. To this day she sees people like me as warmongers. I see people like her as sissies, apologists, and in some cases, self-loathing Jews. Some people would see these disagreements as healthy and a positive reflection of Judaism. Others would see it as destructive. How can Jews defeat those trying to kill us when we are so harsh on each other?

Some faculty members at this Jewish university seemed more committed to political pet causes than actual Judaism. Too often students were allowed to question anything provided they completely agreed with the professors. Opposing points of view were not to be tolerated. This was a university, not a place of higher learning.

In retrospect these people were shaped by their experiences. Mine molded me. I saw the professors as close-minded, but I cannot remember a time when I saw their view of the world as valid. A mirror would have done me some good. While I still maintain that some of the professors went overboard, most of them never had a chance to make a positive impact. I now realize that college is a miserable experience when the student has no desire to be there.

Even under the worst of conditions, contributions to important life lessons can take place. During my junior year of college, a bizarre coincidence was taking place. In 1992, after exactly twenty-nine years, UJ President David Lieber and Chairman of the Board Jack Ostrow were stepping down. In 1992, after exactly twenty-nine years, Johnny Carson and Ed McMahon were retiring from *The Tonight Show*. Many in the community noticed the parallels between these two Los Angeles entities.

The UJ had a very sophisticated business plan. Wealthy donors bequeathing millions needed to die so the university could stay afloat. Ceremonies were held to honor these donors who promised to live long happy lives but not too long. At one of these grovel-fests I saw Chairman Ostrow across the room. Hurtling past other people like a linebacker, I was determined to get to the door before he did. Youth was on my side. I got to the door to open it up for him, and he thanked me. Then came the kissing of his ring.

"Mr. Ostrow, I heard you were stepping down. You, Dr. Lieber, Johnny Carson, all the great ones are leaving."

Mr. Ostrow smiled and gave me a sage piece of advice I carry to this day. "It is always better to have people ask, "Why are you leaving?" than, "When are you leaving?" I laughed as he offered one more thought. "Thank you for opening up the door for me. Perhaps very soon I can open up a door or two for you."

The message was crystal clear, but one hostile woman could not stand to see a young guy succeed his way. Lech Walesa approached me and accused me, quite accurately, of politicking. My mistake was denying it, as if politicking was something to be ashamed of. A telephone call to my father provided a desperately needed jolt of reality.

"Eric, you keep politicking. The Dean already has a job. You need one. She has no interest in helping you and nobody ever got rewarded being too shy to approach powerful people. If I knew then what I know now, like LBJ said, I'd have kissed their (hides) in Macy's window.

The best advice I ever received at the UJ came from an elderly British man named Norman Lee. He and his wife Sadie provided a merit scholarship that covered one hundred percent of my tuition. I never understood why so many Americans despise rich people or demand that they give back more. Everything I have ever gained came from people with more money than me. The Torah does not condemn rich people or condone poor people stealing from the wealthy. Rich people made sure that I earned a college degree without paying one penny for tuition.

Mr. Lee met some of the students at our pre-graduation luncheon. He politely shook hands with the literature and psychology majors and quickly moved on. When I said I was a business major, he put his arm around me and said, "Business, let me teach you some things about business." He took me over to his wife in front of several senior administration officials desperately trying to glue their lips to his posterior. Those frowning over my politicking felt that their own brown-nosing was apparently different.

In front of them all, he asked me if I was getting A's. I told him I was getting B+'s. He cut me off and said, "I want to see A's." Sadie Lee in her gentle voice said, "Now Norman, B+'s are perfectly respectable." In front of everyone Norman looked at me and said, "You are going into business. I invested in you. You were a wise investment. Prove me right." After I replied, "Yes, sir," he offered me the greatest piece of advice I have ever been given. It was advice most Jews will never have the courage to give.

"Eric, don't ever be ashamed about making money. As long as you live life the right way, and you give back, it is a good thing to make as much money as possible. Making money allows you to help people. It makes you feel good and it makes them feel good. Don't ever let people say making money will not make you happy. If you live honorably, it absolutely will."

He then gave me an intense look and said the phrase that will stay with me forever.

"Eric, I'm rich, and I'm happy."

God rest his awesome soul. Too many Jews suffer from needless guilt. Comedians (often Jewish themselves) reduce these Jews to stereotypes of angst-ridden worriers afraid of enjoying their own success. Not every Jew has to be a starving social worker. I was going to be a stockbroker with zero qualms.

To my relief, Dr. Robert Wexler was chosen to lead the UJ in 1992. He was a rabbi but also a businessman. His selection by the board was a sensible admission. Debt is not noble, profits are not greed, and Jewish values do not preclude fiscal sanity. Never send a rabbi to do a businessman's job. In Wexler, the UJ got both.

Another great Jewish life lesson learned from the UJ is that you have to stand for something. During my college years I felt the UJ sadly did not. Academically it was a solid institution. At least the business classes were solid. Philosophically, I felt the UJ was bankrupt. A pair of situations showed what happens when a small university desperate to expand tries to be all things to all people.

The rabbinic students wanted the UJ to be more religious. The undergraduate students like myself were mostly secular. We wanted a Jewish environment but not a yeshiva. The UJ called itself conservative but it was closer to reform than orthodox. Tensions between the graduate and undergraduate students bubbled to the surface when the UJ had to decide whether to have a Halloween dance.

The rabbinic students argued that the UJ was a religious institution. Halloween is a pagan holiday. A Jewish university should not sanction anything practicing Jews refuse to celebrate. The undergrads insisted that they were attending a typical liberal arts college.

Solomon offered to split the baby in half to separate the clear thinkers from what modern society should refer to as thoughtless, heartless imbeciles. The UJ faculty tried to play Solomon. They fashioned a compromise that managed to satisfy nobody.

A dance would be held, but not on October 31. To avoid being seen as a Halloween dance, it would take place on Saturday night, October 30. The change was useless since Saturday night is when UJ dances were held anyway. To avoid the appearance of Halloween, the balloon scheme of orange and black was altered. The proposed dance would have orange, silver and black balloons. The final compromise was that the dance would not be called a Halloween dance. It was to be given a Jewish theme. We were going to be having a "Hal Levine" dance, a celebration of Hal Levine's birthday.

I switched from favoring a dance to opposing one. I knew I had a long way to go before becoming the Jew I needed to be. I also did not need to lie to myself and pretend I was better than I was. Either have a Halloween dance or have no dance at all. Sitting on a fence like Hamlet leads to splinters up the rump.

To my astonishment, history repeated itself in the worst way. A few months later the exact same debate occurred over whether to have a Valentine's Day dance. Insanity is doing the same thing over and over and expecting a different result. Insanity ran wild in the UJ offices. The dance was held on February 13 instead of February 14. Instead of red and white balloons, the dance would have red, pink and white balloons. The Jewish themed event would be the "When Chaim met Sadie: Sadie Hawkins Dance."

Orthodox Jews do not have these dilemmas. The laws are clear. People are free to obey or disobey them. They should not try to play less than clever games to give themselves a false sense of obedience. Obeying the black letter of the law is enough with American law. In Judaism the spirit of the law matters as well.

I now know that declaring the UJ philosophically bankrupt is an overstatement, and an unfair one at that. Being a conservative Jewish institution is like being caught in a vise. The UJ was getting it from all sides. Some Orthodox institutions saw it as Jewish light. Some Reform institutions derided it as too strict. It was also engaged in a public conflict with the Jewish Theological Seminary, another conservative institution.

I was a fledgling boy trying to survive in a world I did not understand. Take those cross-pressures and multiply them many times over. That is what it is like to be a fledgling university trying to succeed. When a university lacks for students, it risks being shut down. Professors fretting about the very livelihood of the institution had little patience with two freshmen alpha males fighting over a girl and a pizza. I criticized the UJ for not picking an exact place on the Jewish spectrum and sticking to it. I now realize that I still haven't picked my place on the Jewish spectrum.

College was not all bad. I made lifelong friendships. We had our share of fun. Besides, the hypocrisy I lampooned could have been spared from my existence had I just engaged in a different dishonest act. My friend Jason had the same last name as the new rabbi for student life on campus. A mail delivery mix-up led to Jason's interesting announcement.

"Hey Eric, according to this document I'm a conservative rabbi."

I was unsure if Jason even knew which if any denomination of Judaism he preferred. Rabbinical school back then was a six-year graduate school ordeal. We were sophomore undergrads. I asked Jason if he sent away for one of those mail order clergy certificates, but neither of us knew if Judaism even has those things. His excitement grew.

"Eric, I've been invited to attend a convention."

Neither of us had been to a convention before. We had no idea what people did at conventions. I remember watching *The Honeymooners* with Jackie Gleason and Art Carney. When their characters Ralph Kramden and Ed Norton went to Lodge Brothers Conventions, there were secret handshakes, funny hats, and parties into the night. Jason said the invitation allowed rabbis to bring guests.

The mail mistake ended up being corrected. Jason and I were forced to continue attending classes in Los Angeles with fellow undergrads. We did not get to attend the convention. While there would have been an adjustment once we found out what a rabbinic convention actually entails, it would have been fun. The rabbis all had funny hats, and so did we. We did not speak a lick of Hebrew but we could have learned. We could have spent the weekend learning Jewish texts. This could have been the beginning of a Jewish lifestyle. It was not to be.

Another sign from above came when it was time to choose classes for our junior year. We were both taking business classes and decided to try something different. We opened up the list of classes, closed our eyes, and decided that whatever we picked at random would be our electives for the next semester. Two fingers waved around and landed on the same spot. Jason and I would both be taking Pentateuch with Rashi.

A thrilled Jason looked and me and asked, "Who is Rashi?"

Nothing would dampen our euphoria as I replied, "I'm not sure. What's a Pentateuch?"

As we sat in adviser Mark Bookman's office, he had the list of classes already prepared. I could barely contain my enthusiasm.

"Sir, I want to take Pentateuch with Rashi."

Without making a facial expression, he put pen to paper and quietly spoke as he wrote, "Business Law II."

I reiterated the desire to take Pentateuch with Rashi. He spoke as he wrote. "Got it. Macroeconomics. Ok guys, have a good semester."

For once, a college professor who thought he knew better than me actually did. Mark Bookman prepared a business major to take business classes to succeed in the business world. While I appreciate his keeping me focused, I missed out on a chance to become the greatest theologian in the history of theology. Kids will not be reading my commentaries in the Jewish community like they do with Rashi and RaMbaM.

Over two decades later, Jason is still not a conservative rabbi. We both eventually attended different conventions where they wore funny hats. Mine was political and I think his involved comic books or animation. Three weeks after graduation I began my stockbrokerage career and never looked back.

One other professor had a profound impact on me. Rabbi David Wolpe is an intellectual titan who would go on to spar with the late avowed atheist Christopher Hitchens. If my brain ever absorbs half of what they learned, I will have done well intellectually.

In my freshman year Rabbi Wolpe taught Ancient Western Civilization. His final exam asked student to determine who was better to run the Roman Empire. On one side were warriors Julius and Augustus Caesar. On the other side were thinkers including Cicero.

I went with Cicero. The pen is mightier than the sword.[3] Trust the writers over the fighters. Warriors could win wars but only the brightest minds could maintain the bureaucracy, keep the civil institutions functioning, and preserve the Empire.

Wolpe gave me an A- instead of an A, explaining that on cold winter mornings he was not interested in what made his car run so long as it ran.

I went to his office and very politely asked him if I could rebut his argument. I would normally never question an A-, but I disagreed with his reasoning. Anyone taking on an intellectual giant had better be prepared.

I pointed out that on cold winter mornings, starting the car was not enough. If the car died, I would need to know how to repair it to avoid being stranded. Wolpe replied, "I have Triple-A."

I was overmatched. Wolpe offered the one rebuttal I could not combat. He told me I was a bright young man and proceeded to end the discussion with an answer as unsatisfying as it was true. "Eric, I'm the teacher, that's why."

He was right. I didn't like that answer. He made matters worse by saying it with such a smile that I liked him anyway. At least I had matured some since third grade. I did not draw a line through my report card to turn the A- into an A+. I think I was grateful he did not downgrade me for my handwriting. My biggest relief was that college term papers were typed. I was a terrible typist but the handwriting nightmares were ancient history. As for Wolpe, he was a rare bright spot at the UJ who soon left.

I relayed the grade story to Hitchens and jokingly requested that he avenge my A- by cleaning Wolpe's clock in their next debate. I told that to Wolpe as well. No such luck. It was a draw. I had much to learn.

After I graduated, history repeated itself. While on campus playing pickup basketball, an Israeli guy who on more than one occasion hassled me decided to up the ante. When he went for a layup, I fouled him. He got angry and forgot that a basketball game is not a violent Middle East war zone. He either suffered from PTSD or was just an anti-social individual. He charged at me, put his hands around my neck, and began strangling me.

People pulled him off me as he continued to scream at me. I lost it and called him a third world savage Israeli dog. I told him that we act civilized in America. If he wanted to be a third world Israeli baboon, he could join the circus and eat bananas.

Life is about learning, and only as an adult does a valuable lesson come into play. Just because person A started the conflict does not mean person B is obligated to escalate. Judaism does teach justice, but nowhere in any Jewish texts does it say that a verbal slight deserves the verbal equivalent of nuclear weapons in retaliation. Diplomacy is not always a waste, but in some situations war is the answer.

I was no angel in school. I had a temper. I was far from perfect. So was the UJ. I went there hoping to get closer to Judaism. I left a disgusted individual with no desire to live a Jewish life. Even more troubling was my newfound hostility to Israel. Only a country as awful as Israel could produce people as vile as Israelis. My coldness toward Israel was offset because I disliked the behavior of the Arabs much more. When told that Israelis were my people, I would angrily reply, "I am American!"

For these and so many other reasons, it was a relief to escape college. I love learning, but school is not for everyone. No occurrence at work was so bad that it made me wish I were back in school. That is why the valedictory speech was so sweet to hear. The valedictorian explained that he chose the UJ because when he was running around the halls of his high school, not many thoughts went through his "usually stoned head." It was the last time a UJ valedictory speech would ever be given without being reviewed by the university first. Future commencement remarks were to be as boring, bland, meaningless and satisfying as a Hal Levine dance.

The UJ pushed me as far away from Judaism as possible, but perhaps that is what I wanted all along. The UJ certainly did not teach me to blame an entire nation for a conflict with one guy over a game. If an Irish Catholic had tried to strangle me I would not have blamed all Irish Catholics. When a radical Muslim commits a terrorist act I do not blame all Muslims. To blame all Israelis for the acts of one bad guy made no sense. That was inside me. Nobody taught it to me. By the grace of Hashem, that attitude passed through me very quickly.

Graduating college led to the real world, where most people are not Jewish. Perhaps it was time to give Judaism another chance. After all, 6,000 years of tradition should not be tarred because of one college institution. So many anti-Israel bigots want to destroy the Jewish state. The last thing Israel needed was one more Jew hostile to the entire country just because of one horrendous Israeli.

I still have strong philosophical differences with the UJ. Having said that, don't ask me to pretend that I speak for the entire student body. I do not represent Judaism. I represent me and me alone. Some students had positive experiences at the UJ. I was probably never cut out for college. I am certainly not qualified to build a university and run it. I would never want me for a student. That first Dean I criticized once asked the class what to call a hypothetical Israeli bombing of every Arab in the Middle East. I snarkily replied, "justified retaliation."

I had a lot to learn. I still do.

Chapter 3: Grandparent Lunacy: No Grandpa, I'm not married

The most powerful influence on a child is his family. That has been true since Adam and Eve ate that apple. Children can survive the worst schools with help from a strong and loving family. My grandparents are my heroes. Judaism was good enough for them, so it had to be right for me. They were Orthodox, which convinced me that my earlier struggles were not with Judaism, but with a half-baked, half-hearted attempt to strip Judaism apart and replace it with some new age nonsense posing as a religion.

My mom's parents were amazing people. Jewish history would be far from complete without them. They were married sixty-seven years, with my grandfather passing away three weeks shy of turning ninety-seven and my grandmother departing three weeks shy of the magic one hundred. Between the two of them, they were around for over three percent of Jewish history.

My favorite Rabbi and Rebbetzin

My mom's father was an Orthodox rabbi. Being the grandson of a rabbi and rebbetzin is something many kids can claim. Being the grandson of this particular rabbi and rebbetzin was fun. They were characters through and through, especially my grandfather.

Before becoming a man of the cloth, my grandfather was a rumrunner. Some of the happiest days of his life were spent running booze during prohibition. He mentioned proudly that he "had more fun than Joe Kennedy."

His youthful experiences may not have aligned with the spirit of Judaism, but he was not a man who one day discovered religion. He was always Jewish and proud of it. His early experiences allowed him to understand the younger generation including his spirited grandson. His advice was wrapped in love, humor, and a speaking manner more suited to a friend than a stern lecturer.

"So Eric, when you get married…you're not married are you?"

He was not senile, but the question seemed crazy.

"No I'm not married Grandpa. Why would you ask me that? Of course I'm not married."

He was crazy like a fox.

"Well I know you're an independent who likes to run off and do things without telling the rest of the family. Anyway, when you get married, carve the date of the wedding into the bedpost. The wedding is the special day where two people become one. It is the holiest of days. Plus, this will keep you when you are old and senile from forgetting your anniversary. No matter how old you are, forgetting your anniversary gets you in trouble. So carve the date into the bedpost so you never forget that special day."

It was a very beautiful idea. I asked my grandfather if he did that to show his love for my grandmother. His message was clear.

"What are you nuts? You think your grandma is going to let me ruin a perfectly good piece of furniture?"

Sometimes in our telephone calls my grandfather would use cryptic language to describe adult topics. The lesson learned would come soon enough.

"Eric, I hear you are seeing a young lady. If there are any *problems*, you let me know. I'll wire you the money so you can have her take care of the *procedure*. I won't tell your parents. The money will arrive and you can handle the matter quietly."

My mind in college was focused on video games. I certainly was not ready for marriage and children, much less the always-delightful dinner topic of abortion. My response was innocent enough.

"Grandpa, doesn't the Torah command people to wait until they get married to have sex?"

The trap was set, and I was the one who fell in it, not him.

"How would you know that? When was the last time you studied Torah my young grandson?"

He recommended rereading it to remind myself not to get any ideas that nice Jewish boys from good families may be tempted to get. As a rabbi, he could perform a wedding on the spot if necessary. Any pending childbirth meant that a wedding would be performed so fast that time would turn backward to make sure everything was kosher.

"Eric, 7 ½ months is perfectly respectable. If she is having your child, we have the wedding immediately. We will tell everyone it was love at first sight. If the child is born 7 ½ months later, we will let everyone know that this child was so ready to be filled with Jewish love that it demanded to be born six weeks early. Kids are born prematurely all the time."

While Judaism allows us to question things, there is no religious law that requires people to ask stupid questions. Halachah is meant to lift us up, not dumb us down. I forgot this on more than one occasion.

"Grandpa, what happens if the baby is born five or six months after the wedding?"

This rabbi had an answer for everything. "Eric, we get on the telephone, call 'Ripley's Believe it or not,'[4] and declare the child a miracle baby."

My grandfather even had business cards that read, "Pastoral Projections." I remember how this seemed dangerously close to the ethically questionable practice of selling indulgences.

"Grandpa, don't you think it's wrong to sell people passes to get into heaven?"

He corrected me. "No Eric, it's wrong for people to buy them. They should know better."

Jewish Lunacy

While I struggled with my Jewish identity, I found out that even an Orthodox rabbi could have dilemmas. Grandpa was a proud Jew and a proud New York Mets fan. He loved baseball. It was tough for him when the Mets had a major game that fell on Shabbos. Most of the time he would do the right thing and miss the game, since VCRs had not been invented yet.

When I visited, my job was to be the heretic grandson who would trip over something and have my nose accidentally turn on the television. This was difficult since the television had a knob. Any Jews involved with the making of the television remote control deserve to be in Jewish history books.

My grandmother would come in the room and say, "Eric, you know better." I would explain that I forgot. She knew full well what was going on. This one time I offered what I considered to be a reasonable justification defense.

"Grandma, he has been punished enough. He is a Mets fan. What more can Hashem do to punish them?"

By keeping the Mets terrible and unwatchable, it kept my grandfather from having Shabbos lapses. 1986 was a tough year. The Mets won the World Series in dramatic fashion. A couple of Havdalah services ran late because of extra innings. Thank Hashem for inventing DVR machines to prevent modern generations from making such painful choices.

Anybody on the 1986 Mets got lifetime immunity from my grandfather for any bad behavior. Grandpa would give sermons about personal responsibility, honor, and avoiding the criminal life. Somehow, no matter what he did, Mets outfielder Darryl Strawberry was always, "just a good kid who needs some love." He and pitcher Dwight "Doc" Gooden could not stay out of trouble. Most people who abused alcohol and drugs were considered to be doing bad things. My grandfather warned me repeatedly not to fall into alcohol and drug use. As for Doc and Straw, they were just good kids who needed some love.

While he may have had a flexible morality on some issues, there was no wiggle room when it came to family. My grandmother and their two children and five grandchildren were his entire world. He performed my Bar Mitzvah and made sure as I got older that I always knew what it meant to be a Jew.

My grandmother was tough. She loved her grandchildren but was not afraid to speak her mind when any of them went astray. One night while visiting my grandmother I stayed out past 4:00 a.m. I was twenty-eight years old, but her home meant her rules. As I quietly put the key in the lock, I remembered one part of her hardwood floor that made a horribly loud creek. Not being terribly coordinated at that hour, my foot stepped right on the creek. I heard her stirring. This was not going to end well.

Even my tired bones when pressured could move faster than a woman of nine decades. As her walker slowly took her step-by-step, I raced to the couch in the living room where I slept. Fully clothed, I covered myself in a blanket and pretended to be sound asleep. She finally reached the living room.

"How nice, my grandson is sleeping like a little angel."

I raised my arms and stretched an exhausted stretch as if she had just woken me up. I smiled at her and mumbled something about being happy to be relaxed and sleeping. With the skill of an Olympic champion, she used her cane to yank the covers off of me. Seeing me fully clothed, the only thing left was to take my medicine.

What made matters worse is that my grandmother kept impeccable records in her notebook. A little over a year later she was in the hospital after having an accident in the apartment. I went to her apartment to get her date book containing medical information. One entry read, "Eric, 4:20 a.m."

She thankfully recovered, so I broached the issue of the entry that should never have been there.

"Grandma, there is something wrong in your date book. You wrote that a few months ago I came home at 4:20 a.m. This is not true. It was 4:10 a.m. You spent ten minutes scolding me."

She was unyielding. "Eric, if you did not come home that late I would not have had to scold you. Not that there will be a next time but if I scold you for an hour that time will count as well."

A few days later my cousin David and I were in the car on our way to a minor league baseball game. "You know Eric, you really came through when Grandma needed you. Thank God you were in the right place at the right time to help her. By the way, did you really come home one night at 4:20 a.m.?"

I was not going to tolerate these false character assassinations. "It was 4:10 a.m.!"

She never changed her datebook and we never agreed on whether a lecture counts toward the time. We did agree that living life the right way a Jewish boy should live is the quickest way to avoid a lecture. More importantly, not everyone has people who care that much. If a child or grandchild of mine ever came home at that hour, there would be a reckoning. I would let them know that they were lucky to only be dealing with me. My grandmother's nickname was "The General."

She had a dry sense of humor. I remember watching television with her a few months before she died. I told her she was my best gal. She asked me if I was sure of that, and I reiterated the sentiment. Without missing a beat, she said, "Well you have a short attention span." After offering the sentiment a third time, my cellphone rang. My girlfriend was on the line, and out came the words, "Hey sweetie, how are you?" My grandmother smiled wryly and said, "There you go." After I hung up the phone she noted that being my best gal was a very short-term endeavor.

I was with her the night before she died. She was fine. She had her hearing, her sight and her mind. We were watching *Deal or No Deal*.[5] I established the ground rules. "Grandma, tonight we are not making any deals. No matter how good it sounds, hang tough." This continued through the commercials. She saw an advertisement for an entire pizza pie for only four dollars. "No deals. Hang tough, Grandma. We're not making any deals tonight with anybody." She laughed and said, "Well you're too hard on people." This was the same woman who refused to alter the infamous ten minutes in her date book. That was one deal she never made.

The next morning I kissed her on the cheek and went to work on Wall Street. I told her that morning I would call her when I got back to Los Angeles. I worked all day, caught my flight, and due to some delays finally got home at 5:00 a.m. My phone rang immediately upon my landing. It was my mother. Her mother had passed away peacefully in that same chair.

Had I stayed in New York, maybe I could have done something. I was the last member of the family to see her alive. Small solace comes from knowing that she immediately ended up in the sky with my grandfather. The angels guarding heaven's palace who travel down to visit Earth better be returning to heaven every night at a reasonable hour.

Chapter 4: Grandparent Lunacy Part II: Yes Grandpa, I got another haircut

My father and his parents are Holocaust survivors. They were on the run for four years in Poland, hunted like animals. Including the three of them, my dad's father saved seven people. After having all his property seized and his parents, siblings and relatives murdered by the Nazis, he came to America and washed dishes. He lived in a one-bedroom apartment and had holes in his socks. You will not read about him in any history book, so this book had to be created. He was made of steel, but always let his grandchildren know how much he loved them. He was a hero, and one of the only Holocaust survivors to consider a real tragedy the length of his grandson's hair.

Honor thy grandfather, cut thy hair

My family was structured like a Mafia family, and my dad's father was definitely at the top of the pyramid. A diminutive man in height, he was a giant of a man in every other way. When he banged his cane, a law had been created. Some people have power. He had moral authority. Try telling a Holocaust survivor what life is about. Try defying a Holocaust survivor's wishes and then look them in the eye.

My parents just wanted me to get decent grades and live an honest life. The length of my hair was never a concern as long as it was neat. My grandfather was tougher. In Eastern Europe, boys looked like boys and girls looked like girls. He was not pleased when I grew my hair long. He never shook the notion that boys with long hair were trouble. One day during my college years he told me that I looked like a "Calderone."

I had no idea what he was saying. He reminded me many times in his thick accent that he spoke five languages: "Russian, Polish, Ukrein (Ukrainian), 'Eedish (Yiddish) and English." To me Calderone sounded Italian. He definitely did not speak Italian. I asked him what language Calderone was. He looked at me and said, "College boy, you don't speak English. I never went to college and I understand English. How do you go to college and only learn one language, and not even understand that one?"

My parents were rarely there when I visited my grandparents, but this time my dad was around to intercede. He conversed with his dad in Yiddish as I wondered why anyone brought children into this world. Finally there was a language breakthrough. My dad made some headway.

"No pop, his name is Calderone. There is no such thing as a Calderone. It's a person, not a thing. Calderone is his last name."

I asked, "Who the heck is this Calderone guy?" My father looked at me and said, "Your grandfather says you look like the drug dealer from *Miami Vice*."[6] My dad watched the show that was up against *Dallas*.[7]

My grandfather never shook that image. When he asked me if I sold drugs, I told him that I had never even tried drugs. As expected, the next words out of his mouth were, "but the hair…"

Enough was enough. "Grandpa. I love you. Listen to me closely. The hair does not make you sell the drugs. I have long hair. I don't do drugs. I don't sell drugs. Nothing in the hair forces you to be involved with drugs."

Things came to a head when my cousin Brian was preparing to have his Bar Mitzvah. I was a college sophomore in Los Angeles, 3,000 miles away from everyone else. I was returning to New York specifically for the Bar Mitzvah. Grandpa's excitement at my pending arrival made him especially loving in our weekly telephone conversation. Then he got to the punch line.

"Eric, it will be great to see you. You make me proud. I love you and am glad you are coming in for the Bar Mitzvah. You will look even more handsome when you get a haircut."

I stopped him with intelligible sounding words followed by an actual question. "Whoa, hey, yo, huh? Whah? Whoa, hey, no. Who said anything about a haircut?"

After explaining to him that I had no intention of cutting my hair, he made it clear that being twenty years old did not make me an adult with any right to make decisions.

"Eric, if you don't cut your hair, you can't come to New York."

This was not true. "Grandpa, you can't ban me from the state of New York. You're not the Governor of New York. You're not the Mayor."

He was unyielding. "Eric, I may not be the head of New York but I am the Grandpa of this family. If you refuse to cut your hair, you cannot come to the Bar Mitzvah."

I explained to him that he could not just kick me out of the family. I had lifetime membership for better or worse. I had every right to attend the Bar Mitzvah. Then he got really tough.

"Eric, you say you can come to the Bar Mitzvah and I cannot stop you. Well maybe I will not come. If you show up looking like an animal, I will not go to the Bar Mitzvah. When everybody wants to know why the head of the family is not there, I will tell them I was ashamed to be in a room with a boy who looks like a girl. I used to have two grandsons and two granddaughters. Now I have three granddaughters and only one grandson. You can go. I will not go."

I promised to call him back and then placed an emergency phone call to the one person who could out-argue my grandfather. My strong-willed dad called him up and said, "Look pop, he's a good kid. He's getting good grades." After something my grandfather mumbled, my dad replied, "I didn't say great grades. He has good grades. They are good enough. No pop, he's not a drug dealer. It's not his Bar Mitzvah. There is no reason he needs to do this."

More mumbling on the other end of the phone ended with, "I'll tell him pop. Talk to you soon." My dad called me back and said, "Well kid, that's the last time I ever try to go to bat for you. I'm fifty years old. Now he's making me get a haircut!"

My dad's hair was not even long, but by taking off a couple inches it would compensate for how long mine had gotten. Collateral damage was getting ugly. I called my grandfather back and explained to him that, "Even if I did the right thing, it would be for the wrong reasons. I would not be cutting my hair for the Bar Mitzvah boy or even because I believed in it. I would only be doing it because you ordered me to do it."

He replied, "Good enough. The Grandpa is happy."

When I made one last ditch effort to keep my hair, he offered up the grandfather of all Jewish guilt trips.

"Eric, I did not want to talk about this, but it may be the last thing I ever ask you to do. Please honor my last wish."

That is a heavy burden for any kid. "Grandpa, are you dying?"

He answered very carefully. "Eric, let's not talk about it. You know I am old and I am not well. I made it to your Bar Mitzvah and I will make it to Brian's Bar Mitzvah."

I flew to New York, went with my cousin Brian and his mom to the barber, and let this Jewish butcher hack off my locks. It was agonizing.

While Brian was the Bar Mitzvah boy, I was the other star grandchild that day. The Bar Mitzvah itself was fun. Later that night came the Bar Mitzvah party. At the party things got surreal. Grandpa showed me off and told everybody how handsome I was. Complete strangers complimented my gorgeous face. I smiled at them while hoping these were rich people who would leave me a ton of money to ease the pain.

Then came the surprises. Grandpa took me aside. "I know this was hard for you. Don't tell your parents, but here is something for you." He gave me $100. I was stunned. This was more money than I was used to seeing, and it represented something powerful. This hardened man actually felt guilty at what he did.

Then my grandmother took me aside. "Eric, I know this was hard for you. I hope this makes you feel better." She gave me another $100. A little bit later on, Grandma took me aside again. "Eric, I know you're a good boy. Here is another $100. Don't tell your parents. It's for you."

Then Grandpa found me again. This was not a man who had much. "Eric, you're a good grandson. Here is another $200. Your parents don't need to know."

Cutting my hair was not fun, but $500 was pretty sweet. I just hoped the Bar Mitzvah boy got more than me. I looked around to see if anyone else was volunteering anything, but $500 was it. My parents always taught me that if people were overly generous, the honorable thing to do is politely refuse their generosity. A $25 birthday gift from my grandparents was one thing. $500 was a lot. I decided that I earned this money and was keeping it.

Then my dad found me. "Son, I need to talk to you."

I excitedly asked him, "You're giving me money?"

My dad replied, "No. Why would I do that? This is not your Bar Mitzvah. Look, I need to tell you how proud I am of you. I know you didn't want to cut your hair. I know it bothered you. I also know how much you love your grandfather. The Bar Mitzvah ritual turns a boy into a man, but being a man is so much more than that. You put aside your own happiness to honor your grandfather on one of the most important nights of his life. All he wanted was for his two grandsons to have the best Bar Mitzvahs in the world. You gave him that with your Bar Mitzvah. Now you gave it to him again by making sure Brian's Bar Mitzvah was perfect. That is what being a man is all about."

A slip of the lip can sink a ship. I was about to send the Jewish Titanic careening. "Well, given his condition…"

My dad immediately cut me off. "What condition?"

Attempts to backtrack failed. "Dad, we don't have to talk about it. It's fine."

With my dad, nothing is fine until he says it is. "Eric, did he tell you he was dying?"

Somebody was about to get in trouble. "He didn't explicitly say that."

Dad was not letting this go. "He implied it, right? Eric, that man has been dying since 1968. He used that trick to get me to take a haircut when I was about your age. I can't believe nearly twenty-five years later he is still pulling that stunt." He looked in Grandpa's direction.

"Pop, get over here now! You told the kid you were dying? LBJ is not President and you are not dying."

The only thing I cared about at this point was that nobody discussed the money. I was not giving that money back. For a supposedly uneducated man, Grandpa was well prepared.

"We're all dying. I don't know when. I'm old. I could go at any minute. My eyes are bad. Everything hurts. I feel like I am dying sometimes."

He walked away as my father explained to me that Grandpa had just run circles around us. When I asked how to prevent that, I was told it would never happen. I was getting a college degree, but street smarts would always triumph over book smarts.

To outfox my grandfather in the future, I needed street smarts. Thankfully the Torah is the best book-smart and street-smart tome ever written. Every year Grandpa would inspect my hair, and every year except for Brian's Bar Mitzvah year, I flunked. Two years before he died, I had flunked inspection thirteen out of fourteen years.

Enter the Jacob and Esau birthright[8] story that has been retold in a plethora of Jewish history books covering the time period before I was born. These books are worth consulting.

Before visiting my grandfather this time, I tucked my long hair underneath my collar. It was quite itchy. His eyesight was not so good. When I went to visit him, he was so happy to see me. He gave me a hug, reached around, and felt only the back of my shirt. Then we sat down and he asked, "Do you think the Grandpa is a dummy?"

After flunking inspection for the fourteenth time in fifteen years, I called him out on his constant insistence that his eyes were bad. He again said, "I can't see." I asked him in front of his daughter (my aunt) and his home caretaker how a man unable to see could tell that my hair was too long. "Grandpa, you have selective blindness." On the rare occasions he was cornered, his rebuttal was, "Don't say this to the Grandpa. I don't want to argue with you. Finished. That's all."

The following year was the last year I saw him. He was one hundred, and would be gone three months later. Flashing back to Brian's Bar Mitzvah, I remembered every detail of that event. As much as it would still bother me, at age thirty-two it was time for another real haircut. He checked behind and inside my collar. For only the second time in sixteen years, I passed inspection. A decade after his death, I can still picture him bragging to people that his grandson looked like a nice young man.

My hair made him crazy. My marital status had him practically foaming at the mouth. He was married to my grandmother for over sixty years. The exact number is difficult to know because the Nazis destroyed records. He sat me down once and told me that it was time for me to get married. I was thirteen, and it was not the Bar Mitzvah present I was hoping for. A few weeks before I turned thirty he really hammered me. "You go out with this girl, that girl, the other girl, another girl, and you never get anything out of it."

This was one conversation no young man ever wants to have with his grandparents.

"Grandpa, I get plenty out of it. Believe me, I am happy with what I get out of it."

He demanded to know what plenty meant, and I made it clear this was one conversation we were never going to have. Since he disagreed, that meant we were having the conversation.

"Eric, I say you get nothing out of it. You say you get plenty out of it. I want you to tell the Grandpa right now what you get out of it."

He promised me repeatedly that he would not get mad. I braced myself for the grandfather of all smacks across the chops. "Grandpa, I sleep with them." He looked at me sternly and said something so shocking that I would not believe it if I did not witness it. "Oh, that's all right then."

I was not sure he heard me, but he did. "Eric, I'm not mad at you. I was young once. I understand."

I thought I was home free. I thought wrong. "So it's ok if I keep doing this."

The fire returned to his eyes. "No! Look, a boy of twenty-one, ok. Even twenty-five is ok. Twenty-eight or twenty-nine, no more. It is time to get married. You were not always a nice boy. Now it is time for you to be one. A man who is not married is a bum."

I asked him for some clarification. "Grandpa, what if I make a million dollars but I have no wife and kids?"

He was unequivocal. "Then you're a bum."

Jewish Lunacy

Only one more dreaded scenario remained. "Grandpa, what if I have a wife and kids but am broke and barely have enough money to feed my family?"

The man did not mince words. "Then you're a nice boy."

Nearly 6,000 years of Jewish history exists because men like my grandfather escaped the worst evil known to man so that Judaism could be extended. That could only continue if nice Jewish boys married nice Jewish girls. When I was visiting Grandpa, I told him I had a date with a girl at 8:30 p.m. He wanted me to change the time to 7:30 p.m. When I told him she was a nice Jewish girl, he thundered, "What kind of girl is out at night at 8:30 p.m.?"

Pointing out that I stay out that late would have made matters worse. The girl found the story adorable and offered to meet an hour earlier.

Even at age one hundred, he was still cantankerous. He asked me if I wanted whiskey with my lunch. I told him I did not drink alcohol. He was his usual accepting self. "Well I'm a man, and I'm going to have some whiskey with my lunch. What is that red (stuff) you drink, the stuff in the refrigerator?"

I normally drank soda, but he was referring to cranberry juice. He turned to his aide.

"Get the boy that red (stuff) he drinks. Get him his boy drink. I'll have my whiskey."

I once needed to use his telephone to make a quick call to my office back in Los Angeles. I did not own a cellphone. He was worried it would cost a fortune. I explained it was a toll-free 800 call. He had never heard of such a thing and asked me why any business would accept the charges and let people call them for free. Broken English notwithstanding, my grandfather could grasp some pretty complicated concepts if they were clearly explained. He understood merchants and customers. I told him that if he was charged a single penny for the call, he could let me know. He told me he would not call me because it was expensive. Beside, I called him every Tuesday. When the bill came, he said his aide could not find a single call. He thought I begged the telephone company to take the call off of the bill to avoid getting in trouble with him. If it came down to it, I would have done exactly that. Thankfully my mother never told him about my teenage 540 call.

Money mattered to him because he had everything taken away from him and his family. He never trusted banks because he feared they would go bankrupt. We told him that did not happen in America and to take the money out of his mattress. He died four years before the 2008 financial crisis. Had he been alive, he probably would have made all of us cancel our bank accounts.

When my parents tried to buy sneakers, he would tell the owner of the store that the material was garbage. Grandpa would haggle over the price and get his discount because the store owner was desperate to get him out of the store and away from the other customers. My parents would then sneak back in the store and pay the difference. They repeatedly tried to explain to Grandpa that Americans do not haggle in stores like that.

My grandfather was not a tyrant or a cheapskate. He loved his family as much as any other man who ever walked the face of this planet. This man of few words told me every Tuesday during our short telephone conversation that he loved me. He never truly got over the fear of having everything taken away from him again. When he came to the house I grew up in on Long Island, my father gave him a tour of the backyard. We had a large inground swimming pool with a water slide and a ton of multicolored Pagoda lights. At that moment my grandfather realized that my parents had the American dream. They owned a house. The government was not going to take it from them. I have never seen him more peaceful.

My dad's mother was the only one of my grandparents who did not make it into her late 90s. She was a kind, calm, quiet woman who did not provide much drama. While she receives much less attention in this book than my grandfather, she was every bit as important. She was completely devoted to her Judaism and to her family.

One Saturday she was having chest pains but did not want to inconvenience anybody with such trivial matters such as life and death. She was having heart trouble, possibly a heart attack. She did not want to ride in a car on Shabbos.

When my dad noticed what was wrong, he nearly hit the roof. He got her in a car very quickly, an action that saved her life. My dad explained to me that it is perfectly acceptable to use a car on Shabbos if the purpose is to save a life. There is no violation. Jews are commanded to save a life when given the opportunity to do so.[9] My grandmother was a holy woman, but it took my dad explaining to her that jeopardizing your own health is against Hashem's will. My grandmother never pulled a stunt like that again.

Like many Jewish grandmothers, mine stuffed me full of food and gave my family more to take home. She made enough chicken cutlets to last a week. Long after my grandparents were gone, I found myself sitting in the park with the rest of the ninety-year-olds. One lady came up to me and said, "Your grandmother, I swear to almighty God, she made the best blintzes on Earth."

Enough time has passed that the people in the park and at the Key Foods would no longer recognize me. Those places remain a peaceful oasis in this world. Most young men would not stick around and listen to a bunch of ninety-year-olds reminisce. They should listen. Elderly people are our greatest treasure. Without them, there is no history at all.

Not many people get to graduate college with all four grandparents alive. Even fewer young people turn thirty and still have three out of four grandparents around. Even in death, my grandparents provide a constant reminder that asking Hashem for anything should come only after thanking him for what he already provided.

Chapter 5: Parental Lunacy: The curse of having normal parents

Hollywood will never make a movie about my parents. They didn't do drugs and they went to work every day. I grew up in a normal middle-class household. My mom was active in the local civic association. My father was a mystery to the local children. They never saw him, so they never believed he existed. The neighborhood kids had all these wild theories about who and what he was. The truth was far less sinister. He worked all week and stayed at home on the weekend. He was tired.

Every once in awhile there would be the equivalent of a Bigfoot sighting. A kid in the area would swear that they saw my dad go outside to get the mail. The parents in the area knew my father existed. They would see him at the mailbox and exchange pleasantries. My father was never social, but he was sociable.

Some of the kids felt bad for me growing up without a father. I kept telling them I had one. He was right inside the house. The other kids never needed to come in my house. There was nothing to do there. We all played outside. My closest friends did not live in the area. They did come over to play with me inside the house and they can confirm I absolutely had a dad. The whole thing was amusing.

My parents are now retired in South Florida along with the rest of the elderly Jews. Nothing has changed. My mom knows every single neighbor. Most of the neighbors have heard she is married to my dad. Neighbors who bother to knock on the door will unravel the mystery. He is right there sitting in his chair watching television. He minds his own business and wishes others would do the same.

While children blame their parents for almost everything, I maintain the same zealousness as my parents regarding our family privacy. Like any child, there were good and bad days growing up. Reliving it serves no purpose. One takeaway from growing up in my house is that I was destined to be completely confused from a Jewish standpoint.

What kind of Jew am I? I have no idea. Hopefully a good one

My father entered this world during the Holocaust. He was only a baby but he remembers every detail. My grandmother used to hide my dad underneath her shirt to muffle his cries. He was four years old when the war ended. At age eight he left Poland with his parents and came to America.

My father does not talk about his experiences, so the grisly details will go with him to his grave. That is his choice. He joined the Army, served his country, married my mom, became a schoolteacher, had a couple of children, bought a house with a lawn in a middle-class neighborhood, and eventually retired. This normal American life never hid the fact that he may not have ever truly escaped the Holocaust. He was in ill health much of his adult life. Perhaps it was from being malnourished as a child living in the woods. Maybe he just drew the short straw. It is to his credit that he managed to maintain a sense of humor.

He entered this world a child of the Holocaust getting shot at. Then he was a Vietnam veteran. Despite being in a non-combat role, he was shot at. Then he was a schoolteacher in the roughest area of Brooklyn. In Bedford Stuyvesant, known as "Bed Sty do or die,"[10] my dad was…you guessed it…shot at. Now he is retired in South Florida where he goes target shooting. The targets do not shoot back.

When you are the son of a Holocaust survivor, you will not get an ounce of sympathy growing up for anything as long as you live. At age fourteen I tried to convince my father that social studies class was too difficult. He looked at me unsympathetically and asked, "Did the teacher try to shoot you?" When I told him no, his next words were, "Get upstairs. Books. Learn. Personal responsibility. No victicrats in this household."

Like many Jews, my father was political. As frustrating as politics can be, he maintained his sense of humor about it all. One time he told me, "Eric, we have got to secure the Florida border." He was over an hour North of Miami, hours from the Florida Keys. At this point there was only one question to ask him. "Dad, what have the Cubans ever done to you?"

His answer was classic. "Son, I'm talking about the Northern Florida border. The New Yorkers keep coming. They bring the bad weather with them."

One of the greatest political dramas played out in the 2000 election between Al Gore and George W. Bush. Palm Beach County introduced the world to pregnant chads. In the Florida Jewish community, that American election was a Jewish story. Palm Beach County is heavily Jewish.[11] Highly educated Jews were confused by the butterfly ballot. Through recount after recount, my dad was amusingly cynical. "Well son, it looks like world peace is finally breaking out."

I asked, "Where are you going with this pop?" He got right to the point.

"To think that elderly Jewish Holocaust survivors are willing to put aside the past, let bygones be bygones, and vote for Pat Buchanan.[12] Son, if your mother and I ever get to the point where we can't figure out a ballot…or we are too feeble to push the thing all the way through…son, at that moment we will have become useless. Euthanize us, the house is yours."

When my parents retired, my father demanded three things from realtors showing them around. The house had to be near a temple community. He would never go, but he wanted that for my mother. There had to be a $2.99 breakfast place in the area because my dad hated getting ripped off. It does not take a genius to fry some eggs and throw in meat and potatoes. The place also had to be nowhere near a golf course because my father disliked golf. He preferred target shooting. One real estate broker explained to my dad that although there was a golf course next door, Florida has liberalized gun laws. He could shoot on his property. My dad asked the broker, "Can I hunt golfers?" When told he could not, he replied, "Next house."

My dad had no patience for self-righteousness, especially from religious people. I remember him yelling at me when I was eight years old. I had just come back from Hebrew school and let him know that he was not the final arbiter in my life. "Hashem loves me and if you yell at me he will take a lightning bolt and strike you down. He is more powerful than you."

My dad actually seemed amused as he sat me down in a much calmer manner than I was expecting. "Son, God can only punish you after you die. Every day until then your (butt) is mine. This is my house. You and I will be in this house for a long time. When we enter God's house one day, we can have that discussion. In my house, God help you if you ever mouth off that way again."

My mom used to make the entire house Kosher for Passover. No good Jewish kid in his right mind would bring non-kosher food and other chametz into a Pesach-ready house. The day before Passover I caught my dad eating non-kosher food. "Dad, don't throw out the garbage inside the house. Mom is about to make the whole house Kosher for Passover. I can throw the garbage outside if you want." The next day came the payback.

I had just finished my last non-Pesach meal at a fast food restaurant. I did not bring the wrappers inside. As I was about to use the bathroom, my dad stopped me.

"Son, what are you doing?"

The answer seemed obvious. "I have to use the restroom."

My dad stopped me again. "Son, go next door to Susan's house (My neighbor was Catholic)."

I told him that made no sense, so he suggested I go in the backyard behind a tree.

"Dad, I'm not an animal. What is going on?" RaMBaM and Rashi were not there to save me.

"Son, did your mom just make the entire house Kosher for Pesach?"

"Yes."

"Son, did you just eat chametz?"

"Yeeeeeessssss."

"Son, you can't take a chametz leak in a Kosher for Pesach bathroom."

My mom caught me walking outside. "Eric honey, where are you going? Pesach is about to start."

Despite being the son of an Orthodox rabbi, my mom obviously did not know halachah. "Mom, I have to go next door and use Susan's bathroom."

She seemed confused and ignorant of how Judaism worked. "Honey is there something wrong with the plumbing? Should I call a plumber?"

It is so frustrating as a kid to have to educate parents on the simplest of things. "Mom, I don't want to take a chametz leak in a Kosher for Pesach toilet."

My mom was so loving and understanding. "Eric, that is the dumbest thing I have ever heard. Where did you hear such nonsense?"

At that point my eavesdropping dad was laughing uncontrollably in his chair. My mom called his name out with a piercing cry. "What are you teaching him?"

As usual my dad had the last laugh. "The little know-it-all comes home from Hebrew school and thinks he knows everything. Kid, your old man out-argued all the yeshiva bochers back when I was young. Now go take a chametz leak and defile your mom's hard work making a Kosher for Pesach bathroom. Then sit down and be quiet."

My father was an absolutist when it came to religion. Either obey all the laws or obey none of them. Don't pick and choose what to obey and then call yourself religious. One day in college my friends and I were in a diner on Passover. The restaurant was not kosher but our effort was there. We ordered a turkey plate and asked the waiter to hold the stuffing. The waiter explained that the stuffing was free, but we did not want it. We would not eat bread on Passover.[13] He offered us cornbread, rolls and other substitutes. We said we could not eat bread because of religious reasons. He looked at my friends and me like we were speaking Greek, which begs an important question. If we were Greeks in Greece, what language would he think we were speaking?

When I told the story to my dad, he offered his typical loving, understanding sentiments. "Son, your effort was worthless. You were in a non-kosher restaurant. The turkey was not kosher. The plates were not kosher. The cola you drank may have been kosher except the soda machine is probably next to where they fry the bacon. I'm not here to burst your bubble, but what you did was a waste of time. Either keep kosher or go eat bacon-cheeseburgers at the diner. Don't do things half-baked and pretend otherwise so you can feel good about yourself."

Thankfully my mom's father the rabbi had a different take. "Eric, I am not telling you to eat at non-kosher restaurants. However, Judaism is not absolute. Do what you can. Constantly learn and strive to improve. Had it not been Passover, you would have eaten the stuffing. Of course giving up the stuffing is a good thing. Never stop making an effort to do better."

My father believed in clarity. Telling the truth was expected. Making your points in a crystal clear manner was demanded. His most frequent refrain was, "Is there a point to this conversation?" Yet when it came to Judaism, the message I received was muddled.

My mother wanted us to be more religious. My father did not. Since he was the Holocaust survivor in poor health, my mom catered to what he wanted. While my father refused to partake in religious rituals, he demanded that his children follow their mother's example.

As my mother would be about to light Shabbos candles, my dad would be in the other room watching television. When I told my mom I wanted to watch TV with my dad, he snapped, "Get in the kitchen and light the candles."

The same man who ate pickled pigs feet told me, "Never forget the core of who you are. You are a Jew." He was agnostic (refusing to ever consider himself atheist, because he always accepted the possibility God existed) but still said, "I am Jewish to the core."

When my grandparents would try to get me married off, my parents would step in and get them off my back. After my grandparents died, my parents switched sides. My father became hell-bent on seeing me married with children. The problem was no woman was ever good enough. Jewish mothers are supposed to nag. In my house the roles were reversed.

When I told him about a girl, the first word out of his mouth was always, "but?" He was convinced there had to be something wrong. "Does she eat Gainesburgers?" That was his way of asking if she was an ugly dog.

One girl was quite lovely, but I nervously mentioned, "Dad, there is something you need to know about her."

My dad was not one to let somebody else finish a sentence when his mind was made up. "She's not Jewish is she?" Attempts to stop the tirade failed. "If she's not Jewish, I don't want to know you. If you marry non-Jewish, you're not my son. Your grandparents and I did not escape the Nazis so you can throw 6,000 years of tradition down the drain. Remember your family name that he fought for and your great-grandparents died for. If you marry a goy, don't come in my house again."

At this point he had to be stopped. "Dad! Go in the other direction!"

He paused briefly before asking, "Oh. You mean she's very Jewish?"

I corrected the terminology. "Dad, it's called Orthodox."

He then reached out with compassion and understanding. "What do you want that kind of life for? You're going to have to use separate plates. You won't be able to watch your ballgame when you want. You won't come in our house because the food won't be good enough. Why can't you find a nice Jewish girl who is not religious like everybody else?"

If a cure for cancer came out, my dad would probably lament all the doctors it would put out of work. Despite often being impossible to deal with, he got the biggest things right. He never lied to me. He made five or six promises to me in my entire life and he kept them. He once said about me that, "If the kid tells me there are Martians on the roof, I don't have to look. I know they are there." That goes both ways.

He rebelled against religion as a teenager because it was forced upon him. He told me I could make my own decisions when I became an adult. As a kid I listened to my parents. When I pointed out that he did not obey the religious traditions, he offered some powerful advice. "Just because I do something doesn't make it right. Your mother is right. Follow her example."

One other thing about my dad is that if you out-argued him with logic, he would back down. Since he decided what was logical, this almost never happened. One time when I was nineteen he asked, "Why do you act so sophomoric?" I was in my second year of college and proudly replied, "Dad, I am a sophomore." He occasionally conceded that point until I became a junior. Sometimes to get around it he would say, "I meant a sophomore in high school."

My dad had open-heart surgery when he turned forty-eight. We thought we were going to lose him. He survived, and a few weeks after the surgery shocked everyone by showing up in shul during Rosh Hashanah and Yom Kippur. He had not been inside a synagogue in thirty-one years. He took me aside and said, "Don't expect this to be a habit. I just wanted you to know that I know there are forces on Earth more powerful than me. I'm here to thank God for letting me live."

I am not sure he has been in a synagogue since, but twenty-five years after his first of many health scares, he is still thankfully around. For those who think their parents complain too much, the alternative of not having parents is far worse.

My father played the role of complainer. My mother was not your stereotypical mom. She never nagged me or complained about anything. Every Jewish boy thinks his mother is a saint. Mine might be. She visits sick patients in the hospital. She spreads happiness wherever she goes. She even makes my dad smile, not an easy task. Ask her where she wants to live, and she says, "Wherever your father lives." As for what girl I should marry, outside of the girl being Jewish, there are no other concerns. "Honey, I just want you to be happy." She means it.

This does not mean she was always patient, especially when her darling son stretched her patience. At the grocery store I had octopus hands. As fast as

I could shovel stuff into the cart, she could put it back on the shelf. She explained that anything lacking the official K for kosher or O-U for Orthodox Union should not go into the shopping cart.[14] She was not pleased when I put bacon-flavored crackers in the cart. She was even less pleased when I insisted they were kosher.

She was incredulous when I tried explaining that bacon-flavored was not the same as actual bacon.

"Eric, what do you think bacon-flavored is flavored with?"

I pointed out that Bacos were fake bacon bits and they were kosher. She laid down the law. "Bacos have an O-U on them. These crackers do not." I showed her that they did, and then she had finally had enough. "Eric, that is not an O-U. That is O-C, which means the product is copyrighted. It has nothing to do with kashrut and turning the box sideways does not make it kosher."

Her exasperation was complete when I made a phone call to place the weekly order of newspapers I needed to deliver for my paper route. Telephone numbers beginning with 976 are now synonymous with adult phone calls, but back then 976 numbers were used for innocuous information including weather and sports scores. The dirty numbers started with 540 and 550.

The number for Newsday was 454-2000. I mistakenly dialed 540-2000. My mom could not figure out why my face alternated between shock, confusion, and smiling. "Mom, the woman on the other end of the phone likes me. She keeps calling me *sailor* and she is not talking about boats."

My mom flipped out. "Eric, hang up the phone now!"

This was the best call I had ever heard. They did not teach this in Hebrew school. "Mom, she really likes me a lot."

Maybe she was not Jewish, because my mom did not let me get to know her better. "Eric, right now!" My mom grabbed the phone, listened in disgust for less than five seconds, and slammed the phone down. One month later I heard a shriek in the living room. The phone bill had arrived, and that one-minute phone call cost twenty-five dollars. My mother is normally a calm person, but she could barely contain herself trying to explain the mistake to the A T & T operator. "My son is an idiot!" Thankfully the operator had a teenage son herself. The charge was wiped off as my mother assured the operator this would never ever occur again if I wanted to live.

"Eric, do I have to teach you how to dial a telephone? Do you know the difference between four and five?" I looked at her and beamed proudly. "One, mom! Like Hashem! One is Hashem, one is Hashem, one is Hashem, through the Heaven and the earth!"[15]

For a woman who loved Judaism, she certainly did not take joy in my singing a song of praise extolling the virtues of the holy one, blessed be he. At least my mother did not curse Hashem or me. Her harshest criticism was, "You are a dope! Be quiet!"

For a woman who was good at math, maybe she thought the difference between four and five was not one. After all, much of Judaism is subjective. What is not subjective is that I love my parents very much.

Chapter 6: Palestinian Lunacy: A rich history spanning almost 45 years

Jews have existed for nearly 6,000 years. Palestinians have been around for almost forty-five years. This is not a political book. The Jewish community is divided on how to solve the problems in the Middle East. That being said, an honest conversation requires honesty based on empirical evidence that is physical, archaeological and chronological. Feelings and emotion are no substitute for facts. Facts are not treated as such just because somebody types the word *fact* in all capital letters on an Internet message board with exclamation points after it.

I have taken flack for referring to Palestinians as *Palesimians*. For those offended by my words, innocent Jews being blown to Kingdom Come by the most defective members of the Arab community is what offends me. People who let their emotions overrun logical reasoning miss my larger points. To prevent this, I will grit my teeth and not use that term for the rest of this book. I was going to write a book on Palestinian contributions to world history, but most people will not pay for an entire book of blank pages. Ok, back to showing the *restraint* that Jews are constantly being asked to exercise. Herewith is the serious Palestinian contribution to Jewish history.

Palestinians, Unicorns, Eastern Mumbekistan and France

To understand the Palestinians, it is necessary to dispense with politically correct nonsensical platitudes. Here are some phrases with the appropriate transliteration.

"Not everybody who criticizes Israel is an anti-Semite."

Transliteration: Many people use criticism of Zionists as a fig leaf to hide anti-Semitism. They deserve to be called out for what they are.

"I do not hate Jews. I hate Zionists."

Transliteration: You're an anti-Semite.

"Not all Arab Muslims are terrorists."

Transliteration: Virtually all terrorists are Arab Muslims. Timothy McVeigh was a statistical aberration.

"Some Palestinians truly want peace. They want to be free."

Transliteration: Freedom is something people fight and die for. Americans did it in the American Revolution of 1776. When the Arab Spring broke out, the people of Libya overthrew Moammar Khadafi Duck. The people of Egypt had to act twice, taking down Hosni Mubarak and Mohammed Morsi. Some revolutions fail. China put down the uprising in Tiananmen Square. Syria lost over 100,000 people in an attempt to oust Bashar Assad.[16] Young Persians rose up in 2009 only to see the United States refuse to help them, a victory for the mullahs. At no time have the Palestinians ever fought for their own freedom.

"The poor, suffering Palestinians…"

Transliteration: Poverty does not cause crime or terrorism. Plenty of poor people obey the law while plenty of rich people violate the law. The problem is a poverty of values.

"Not all Palestinians are Hamas or Hezbollah."

Transliteration: An overwhelming majority of Palestinians in Gaza voted for Hamas.[17] White Southern support for the Ku lux Klan never reached levels that high. When Klansman David Duke ran for President and then Governor of Louisiana, he was roundly rejected.[18]

"Palestinians did not vote for terror. Hamas builds schools and roads."

Transliteration: The KKK also built civil institutions. They took children to libraries, museums and other cultural places. This is irrelevant. Once even a tiny part of a group's platform includes setting innocent people on fire, all good deeds are invalidated. Try telling Orthodox Jews that a Holocaust denier running for office is mitigated by his support for child tax credits for religious schools.

Saddam Hussein wrote poetry and Adolf Hitler was a painter. They were both genocidal madmen. At least voting for Saddam was compulsory. Hitler and Hamas won democratic elections, which reflects on their people at that time. Anyone who finances, shelters, harbors or supports terrorists in any way is every bit as much a terrorist as those actually planting the bombs or launching the rockets.

"Cycle of violence…"

Transliteration: There is no moral equivalence between terrorists trying to murder a neighboring people and those other people trying to defend themselves and not be murdered. When Palestinians briefly stop attacking, everyone lives.

"Disproportionate use of force…"

Transliteration: War is awful. There is no obligation to have an equal number of people die on both sides. Ending a war by winning it is the quickest way to prevent more deaths. President Harry Truman dropped atomic bombs on Hiroshima and Nagasaki. While it was tragic that thousands of innocent Japanese people died, this ended the war and saved many more lives. Collateral damage is unfortunate but can never be a deterrent. Collateral damage during war does not require any apology of any kind. The Maccabees understood how to win wars. Only idiots would deliberately start a conflict with a superior military and purposely get their own people killed to win a public relations war. In recent years a football game saw one team humiliate the other team 58-0.[19] The losing team could have gone to the United Nations and claim that the winners should have stopped at 10-0. The additional touchdowns were not necessary. The winning coach could have been brought up on human rights abuses, but since he was not Jewish the matter was dropped. The losing team had the choice to stop fighting altogether or resume fighting when they had better players.

"The international community…"

Transliteration: The international community is worthless. The United Nations is morally bankrupt. The Holocaust happened because the world let Jews be murdered. The international community failed to prevent genocide in Rwanda, Sudan and Syria. The international community holds expensive conferences on climate change while human beings are being slaughtered around the globe. The Jews have always had to fight for their own existence. The twenty-first century is no exception.

"Humiliating checkpoints and blockades…"

Transliteration: Palestinian terrorist groups including Hamas keep trying to murder Israelis. The restrictions have drastically reduced Palestinian suicide bombings and the smuggling of weapons. Every time Israel eases the restrictions, Palestinians rearm and terrorize. The fact that most Palestinians are not terrorists is irrelevant. The restrictions are necessary to save Israeli lives.

"Refugees and Right of return…"

Transliteration: This is by far the most pernicious attack on Jews disguised as compassion. People fleeing their country under valid circumstances such as war earn the refugee status classification.[20] My father and his parents fled Poland during the Holocaust. They could be given refugee status and the right of return to Poland if they desired. I am a Holocaust survivor's son, which means absolutely nothing from a refugee standpoint. I grew up in New York and have never been to Europe. My father would be eligible for reparations. I would not nor should I be.

The Palestinians are the only people in the world who count the children and grandchildren of people who fled Egypt and Jordan as refugees with a right to return.[21] Ironically, they want the right to return to Israel where they never lived rather than Egypt and Jordan where they did live. Even if the first generation had proof of fleeing Israel proper, the children and grandchildren would have no such claim. The only motivation for this special invented refugee status is to flood Israel with as many Palestinians as possible to destroy Israel as a Jewish state internally. If a grandfather sells his house in California to pursue an oil job in North Dakota, his grandchildren cannot seventy years later knock on that California door and demand entry just because they want to sit by the pool all day and avoid freezing winters.

Jews and Palestinians must be judged by the exact same metric that every other people are judged by. Since no other people except for Israel are ever criticized for using disproportionate force, it is reasonable to conclude that this line of thinking is a cover for Jew-hatred.

In analyzing Palestinian history, I must confess my close-mindedness about this subject. I remember the first time I drove from Houston a couple hours North. My heart stopped when I saw the sign welcoming me to Palestine, Texas. I kept the windows up and I did not stop for gas until reaching the next town. Palestinians complaining about the Gaza Strip should be reminded that they have land between Houston and Tyler containing plenty of oil.

Lebanon, Pennsylvania contained some nice people. None of them supported Hezbollah or detonated bombs during my visit. On the downside, this Eastern Pennsylvania city did not contain any of the beautiful cedar trees referenced in the Torah.

One Jewish lesson learned from my travels throughout all fifty states in America the Beautiful was to never rely on a Palestinian GPS tracker. I took one wrong turn, ended up at a cemetery, and heard this sinister machine tell me in a menacing voice that, "You have reached your final destination!" I angrily threw the thing out the window, which was good because five seconds later it exploded.

Most people offended by that remark are Jews claiming it is unfair to lump all Palestinians together. These Jews tell me that perhaps the joke should be changed to a Hezbollah GPS tracker.

Perhaps the Palestinian people should stop voting for Hamas. Jews are far too quick to engage in self-censorship. Every culture has been the subject of jokes at their expense. Only Arab Muslims respond to those jokes by committing violence. Ironically, this validates the jokes since they are about the Arab Muslim propensity to commit violence. The Palestinians have been one of the worst offenders of this violence. Nobody disputes that this violence exists. The argument even among many Jews is whether Palestinian violence is justified.

As Israel is frequently forced to defend itself from Hamas-fired rockets, a peaceful resolution to the Israeli-Palestinian conflict seems remote. Palestinians insist that the rocket fire will not stop until illegally Zionist-occupied Palestine is returned to the Palestinian people. Palestinians claim that they are indigenous to the land and that Israeli colonizer settlers kicked them out. Israel claims that the land has always belonged to the Jewish people.

Most people in the United States find the Palestinian position indefensible. Yet pockets of support for Palestinians can still be found among college university professors and in Hollywood. Since Hollywood celebrities and university professors rarely have their opinions challenged, it is easy for them to remain in their protective cocoons. Once these people have their beliefs questioned, it is easy to make their arguments crumble.

Any individual anywhere in this world who supports the Palestinians over the Israelis must be confronted with two basic questions.

The first question is historical. Who is the father (or mother) of the Palestinian people?

The first human male was Adam. From his rib came Eve, the first human female. The first Jew was Abraham, son of Terah and father of Isaac. The first Christian was Jesus Christ. The first Muslim was Muhammad. These people existed. There is no dispute. Muslims take pride in memorizing the birth of their religion in 622 A.D.

Who was the first Palestinian? When and where was that person born?

Nobody can answer this question. Yasser Arafat became the leader of the Palestinian Liberation Organization in 1970 (some sources say late 1969), but he was an Egyptian by birth.[22] He was only the third PLO leader, since that organization began in 1964.[23]

Which Jew stole the land and which Palestinian did the Jew steal it from? How can any indigenous people struggling for their place in history fail to recite with certitude what that history even is or when it occurred?

George Washington was the Father of his country, the United States of America. He led a war against the British in 1776. Lord Cornwallis led the defeated army who lost the land. In 1789 Washington became the first President of the United States.

What battle saw the Palestinians lose their land? Who led the losing army? If they were displaced, who displaced them? What was the name of the victorious Jewish general?

The reason Palestinians cannot answer questions about their history is because this history is nonexistent. A band of rebel fighters were kicked out of Egypt and Jordan for trying to overthrow those governments. Jordan massacred thousands of them in one day in 1970.[24] Arabs killed other Arabs. The Arabs who fled then tried to take over Israel because it was the one area of the region where they would not be indiscriminately murdered. Rather than accept the role of gracious guests, they tried to seize the land of a Jewish people who had a multi-thousand year documented history.

The second question about the Palestinians is geographical. They claim their land is being occupied. Exactly what land is being occupied?

The Gaza Strip is not occupied. Since 2005, there have been precisely zero Jews living in Gaza.[25] The West Bank could be an answer, but evidence points against this. In 2000, Arafat was offered all of Gaza and ninety-seven percent of the West Bank as part of a peace deal.[26] He turned the deal down because that still would not have ended the occupation.

Palestinians have made it clear that Jerusalem is the capital of their Palestine. At anti-Israel marches they chant, "From the river to the sea, Palestine will be free."[27] From the river to the sea encompasses all of the land. The Arabs have for decades talked about driving the Jews into the sea. This Palestinian goal is completely consistent with Arabs before them.

This is why a lasting peace is impossible. The Arabs were offered two states living side by side in 1948. The Jewish state of Israel would be next to the Palestinian state of Palestine. The Arabs rejected the deal and waged the first of many wars so they could seize all of the land.[28] The Palestinians of 2015 are no different from the Arabs of 1948. These displaced Arabs have convinced themselves that they are entitled to all of the land. The very existence of Israel and its Jews is what they reject.

Palestinians keep demanding an end to the occupation by speaking in generalities. They know that admitting their specific aspirational goals of killing all of the Jews would reduce their public relations support. Even Hollywood celebrities and university professors do not wish to see another anti-Jewish Holocaust.

Palestinian supporters who base their views on Jew-hatred cannot be reasoned with. For Palestinian supporters who are ignorant rather than malicious, ask them the questions.

Who was the first Palestinian? What exact stretch of land do they claim as being occupied?

Until these questions are answered, the Israeli position and its archaeological evidence is the only valid view. Israel is the land that traces back to Abraham, the very first Jew. It is the land of the Jewish people. There were no Palestinians

Jewish Lunacy

in existence then, and the current name used by these displaced Arabs is one of sheer fiction.

Palestinians will yell and scream about Jihad, infidels, and evil Zionists, but they will never be able to adequately answer the two questions relating to their non-existent identity and their malevolent genocidal purpose. For all we know, Palestinians were created when a unicorn had an inappropriate relationship with Sesame Street's Snuffalupagus. Palestinians could have grown up in fictional countries like Eastern Mumbekistan or France. They never lived in Israel. They never lived anywhere before 1970. For forty-five years, they have tried to invade another nation.

The idea that not all Palestinians hate Israel and the Jews is utterly irrelevant. One Palestinian feeling this way is one too many. A plurality is frightening. A majority is sickening. Hamas is indistinguishable from the Palestinian people. The Palestinian people elected a horrible government. While many other peoples throughout history including other Arab groups chose to stand up and fight for their freedom, Palestinians chose to stand down. Palestinians have accepted being citizens of a Hamas terrorist area. Either they lack the basic desire to be free that every other bunch of human beings possess, or they support the aspirational goals of the people ruling them.

If Palestinians had any decency, they would overthrow Hamas. They would risk their lives and take to the streets against their actual oppressors, not some neighboring people simply trying to be left alone in peace. They would not celebrate in the streets and hand out candy to children after America suffered the September 11 attacks.[29] They would not dance jubilantly and fire victory rockets into the air after the Space Shuttle *Challenger* burst into flames[30] (One of the seven NASA astronauts was Jewish).

The worst Palestinian sympathizers shed crocodile tears over the Palestinian ch-ch-ch-ch-children. This is hypocritical. Children are dying all over the world in much larger numbers. Only Palestinian children get special sympathy status that could be described as disproportionate.

Children of KKK supporters receive little sympathy. Few tears are shed when their parents are killed. People choose to support good or evil. A moral conscience must trump everything else.

Dead Palestinian children are a tragedy because any children dying are a tragedy. The question to ask is why they are dying. The answer makes anti-Israel elites and even some Jews uncomfortable, but it must be said. Palestinian children are the victims of terrible parents. Only terrible parents would vote for such a terrible government.

Because the Palestinian conflict with Israel is different from every other conflict, the United States has the latitude to take an approach that would fail everywhere else. There are those who want to build Mother Russia into the former U.S.S.R. Iran wants to dominate the entire Middle East. ISIS and other groups want to establish a global Islamic Caliphate. Israelis and Palestinians are arguing about a confined space.

Neither party wants to take over Jordan, Egypt, Saudi Arabia or Lebanon. The fight is not about power and expansion for the sake of power and expansion. Both sides believe the same small slice of land belongs to them. Neither side wants to expand the conflict beyond Israel proper and the Israeli territories of the Gaza Strip and West Bank. The fight is contained and will stay contained. Because this tiny regional conflict has zero possibility of becoming a global conflict, the United States and the rest of the world should stay out of it.

The next time Palestinians declare a Day of Rage,[31] just look bemused and ask the Passover questions. Why is this night different from all other nights?

Here are some other questions, answers and musings to this temper tantrum for the sake of temper tantrums.

Is the Palestinian Day of Rage based on the lunar or solar calendar? Can Gaza shoppers begin at sundown or midnight? Are discounts on rocket launchers not until the Jewish Sabbath or can they start rearming one day earlier during the Muslim holy day? Will the rage be televised or is this an event so typically boring that like a political speech we can just read the transcripts? Will there be a point to this rage or will people angry at anything and everything just demand free stuff now without knowing why they want it? Are repressed Palestinians still using tunnels to smuggle copies of "Debbie does the Gaza Strip?" or "Yasser Arafat milks his goat?" Once *CNN* leaves, will Palestinian children used as human shields be given right of return by Hamas to the prop department?[32]

Palestinians are always complaining. Suicide bombers are so depressing. They really take the fun out of fundamentalism. What Jews have learned over nearly 6,000 years and Palestinians have failed to learn during forty-five years is that the best way to build a thriving civilization is not to blow it up with dynamite.

Chapter 7: Secular Lunacy: Orthodox Jews get virtually everything right

Reform, Conservative, Orthodox and Reconstructionist Jews are all Jews. I do not believe in labels. I am Jewish and leave it at that. I am as comfortable making friends in a Chabad House as I am in a Hillel House. While they are all good people, the Orthodox Jews are the last best hope to preserve the traditions. For centuries, all Jews were Orthodox. Reform Judaism started as a rebellion against Orthodoxy.[33] Conservative Judaism began when some Reform Jews felt the pendulum swung too far in the other direction.[34] Then came compromises such as Conservadox. Reconstructionist Jews are a separate group entirely.

Non-Orthodox Jews often tell Orthodox Jews to adapt to modern times. It is Orthodox Jews who fought the survival struggles for most of Judaism's 6,000 years. The other sects cannot be faulted for not existing, but credit has to be given to those who kept this religion going.

Orthodox Jews got plenty of things right long before the other sects came along. This longevity gives Orthodox Jews a certain wisdom that at the very least makes them worth hearing out. If I want to learn how to preserve a religion, I will go to the people who have been doing this since the religion's inception.

We were once all Orthodox, and may be again

All Jews should be cherished. Reform Jews have a valid point when they say that without Reform Judaism, there may not be that many Jews left. With sixty to seventy percent of Jews being Reform, it would not be wise for any Jew to face the ultimatum of choosing Orthodoxy or nothing. It is also unfair to automatically assume that Reform Jews are secular. Plenty of Reform Jews keep kosher and Shabbos and proudly live a Jewish lifestyle.

Orthodox Jews are right when they point out that having an organ in a synagogue violates Shabbos. The line that must not be crossed is declaring that people attending musical Friday night services are not practicing Judaism. Given the fifty-two percent intermarriage rate,[35] it is better that Jews attend any synagogue than completely abandon their affiliation.

Too many Reform Jews have also made the mistake of seeing most Orthodox Jews as zealots. Orthodox Jews are strict in how they live their lives, but they are open, warm and tolerant in greeting others.

Despite my not living a strict Orthodox lifestyle, Jews like myself who value empirical evidence can see the truth. The Orthodox get virtually everything right.

What is everything? Since Jews like to answer a question with a question, the real question is different. What matters? What matters is family.

Orthodox Jews by and large in every metric have more successful families. The American divorce rate is around fifty percent. The Orthodox Jewish divorce rate is much lower.[36] Yeshiva students are much happier and healthier than their public school counterparts. They are less likely to be stabbed to death or shot over a pair of sneakers. Yeshiva students get a solid religious education but also excel in mathematics and the sciences. The Orthodox Jewish community is far less likely to see their children abuse drugs. Alcohol is prevalent for religious ceremonies, but fruit of the vine allows grape juice to be substituted for wine.

The Orthodox community is divided between the Modern Orthodox communities and the traditional Chasidic communities exemplified by Chabad Lubavitch. The Chasidic really know what they are doing, especially when it comes to marriages.

Some non-Orthodox people scoff at the idea of arranged marriages. I am not an expert in them myself. I think in the thirteenth century the male gave the female's eldest living paternal relative some livestock in exchange for his daughter's hand. There is no archaeological evidence showing that brides were exchanged for cold cuts, but most men cannot resist cold cuts. There is very little that cannot be exchanged for cold cuts. Gold rises and falls in price, but cold cuts are always delicious. This is why the owner of a Jewish deli is considered a greater catch than a doctor. That could also be fictional, but if it gets passed down as an oral tradition, so be it. While trading pastrami for a wife may not be the 5775 approach to marriage, there is little question that arranged Orthodox marriages are overwhelmingly successful.

Rarely has the secret to something so important been available for everyone to see and yet still get ignored. Orthodox marriages work because both individuals are devoted to Hashem first. While secular people love to find examples of religious hypocrisy, there are plenty of people who live the way they believe and practice what they preach, if they preach to others at all.

Most relationships start with a physical attraction. Are they blonde or brunette? Are they short or tall? Are they thin or fat? Are they good in bed? Then come other intangible externalities. What do they do for a living? How much money do they make? What kind of car do they drive? Do they own a house?

When people bond over a common love of worshipping Hashem and studying Torah, everything else becomes secondary. How do so many Chasidic families have so many children and still provide financially for them? If you ask these parents, they will say that Hashem provides for them and they are blessed. How do these many Chasidic children all turn out to be solid citizens? Children guided by Hashem have an extra incentive to turn out this way.

Many people will not steal from a store because they fear getting arrested. Most people who avoid committing adultery are afraid of getting caught and being subjected to a messy divorce. In the Orthodox world, the Ten Commandments are sacred. Stealing and adultery are crimes against Hashem. That is a heavy burden to bear. When two people both believe that God comes first, they are on the same page from a values standpoint.

Another major aspect of Orthodox married life is the concept of separation. During the eleven days of the month when the woman is considered unclean, the husband and wife sleep in separate beds and refrain from sex.[37] This forces the couple to communicate on other levels. Many secular marriages will see couples fight and then use sex to paper over deep problems. By restricting sex for eleven days every month, Orthodox couples learn about each other in ways that can only be done through conversation.

None of this is to denigrate those living non-Orthodox lives. I live a non-Orthodox life and am as far from self-hating as it gets. One can be non-Orthodox and still lead an honorable, ethical life. One can even be an atheist and live a noble life. Being Orthodox does not guarantee success, but it does give its adherents a much better chance at success.

The best way to lead a fulfilling life is to place energy into something positive. Religious people are more likely to give to charity, help those in need, and spread love. This provides joy to the giver and the receiver, which spreads happiness.

Every life will have its share of pain. Studying Torah cannot prevent pain. The Torah is filled with stories of pain. What the Torah can do is provide a valuable blueprint on how to handle pain.

Rabbi Mendy Cunin of Chabad in Los Angeles taught me the words of the Rebbe Maharash, who spoke of obstacles. People could try to go underneath or around obstacles, but the Rebbe Maharash tells us we must go over the obstacle. The Rebbe Maharash says Hashem puts obstacles in front of us specifically to see if we can jump over them.[38]

The worst obstacle any person can have is to lose a child. Every parent's nightmare is to see their child predecease them. More than one Chabad rabbi I know has lost a young child. They were able to preserve their marriages and still be good fathers to their remaining children. They were still able to be a rabbi to their congregants depending on them. These rabbis were not born superior or impervious to pain. What they do have is complete faith and trust in Hashem.

This unquestioning faith creates an unshakeable resolve that creates unbreakable bonds between man and God, man and woman, and man and child. When I find myself straying down the wrong path, I stop by the local Chabad House and remind myself what truly matters.

It is easy to take advice from people who get virtually everything right. The hard part is taking an undisciplined life and making the hard but right choices. Orthodox Jews understand that it is not about being righteous, or even right. It is about doing right. The most important thing the Orthodox community does right is make sure that Judaism is passed down.

Proud Jews come from all the sects, but Reform Jews are having fewer children. Many of those children are marrying outside the faith. Orthodox Jews, especially Chasidic ones, have very large families deeply committed to preserving the faith. While Orthodox Jews make up only ten percent of Jews overall, the rapid disparity in birth rates means that Orthodox Jews should close that gap.

The ideal situation would be for all sects to increase their birthrates so that there are more Jews in totality. The ideal is not the reality. Orthodox Jews were once the only Jews in existence. That could be the case again. Reform Jews would have only themselves to blame if they sterilize themselves out of existence by refusing to be fruitful and multiply.

My father has lamented to me on more than one occasion that, "What Hitler failed to do to us, we are doing to ourselves through intermarriage and assimilation." Thankfully for all Jews, Orthodox Jews are determined to preserve Judaism forever.

On issue after issue, the Orthodox just get it. Perhaps those religious books they keep reading obsessively are worth even more than we can all possibly imagine.

Chapter 8: Sexual Lunacy: How I became Shomer Negiah

The Jewish concept of Shomer Negiah means that men and women do not touch each other before marriage.[39] Even holding hands is prohibited. In junior high school I was Shomer Negiah. In college, girls finally started talking to me. According to my rabbi, Shomer Negiah is supposed to be voluntary. One cannot violate other Jewish laws and claim to be Shomer Negiah simply because achieving physical attention from females is a lost cause.

I may have described this entire chapter in the above paragraph. Shomer Negiah, or in my case the lack of it at the slightest possible opportunity, has played a key role in my Jewish (some would say lack of) development.

If we had self-control, Hashem would not have created the Mechitza

A famous Orthodox Jewish joke says that premarital sex is prohibited because it could lead to sins like mixed dancing.[40] The concept of Shomer Negiah is based on the slippery slope argument. Even something as innocuous as holding hands can lead to further touching which could then lead to full-blown premarital sex. To cut off this possibility at the source, men and women are segregated.

In the Chasidic world, men and women do not sit next to each other while eating. They sit across from each other, close enough to converse but not touch. Men pray on one side of the synagogue separated from the women. A physical divider known as a mechitza prevents the two genders from even seeing each other.[41] Praying rather than socializing remains the focus. Congregants bond with Hashem first and foremost.

Critics of Shomer Negiah say that it reduces human beings, particularly men, to savage animals who cannot control themselves. Critics must answer a simple question. What evidence in two million years of humanity disputes this theory?

Rabbi Shmuley Boteach, author of the book *Koshersex*, teaches that lust is more powerful than love. If General David Petraeus, the most disciplined man on the planet, could fall victim to lust, what man is immune?[42] Boteach teaches that in healthy marriages, men lust after their wives.

The difficult part is dealing with lust before marriage. Adam was tempted by Eve. He ate the apple. They both got naked and then ended up angry at each other. Men have been lusting after women ever since.

Ask most non-Orthodox single Jewish men why they go to synagogue, Jewish dinners, or other Jewish parties. They want to meet a nice Jewish girl and get married. There is no loyalty to any one synagogue. Guys use social media to discover where the action is on any given Friday night. The determining factor on which service to attend often revolves around which one has the largest crowd and the prettiest girls.

The mechitza exists in Orthodox shuls because the men want to look at the women. Many men have taken a peek, sneaking in quick glances. The mechitzas were then built higher.

Orthodox women dress modestly to avoid being viewed as sex objects. That helps a little, although classy, dignified Orthodox women are among the hottest women on the planet.

At Orthodox Jewish weddings, the men dance with each other and the women dance with the other women. A divider separates the groups. The only time they are joined is when the bride and groom are lifted up in separate chairs high in the air like a queen and king. The people not holding those chairs stand around and clap. There is no physical touching.

Orthodox Jews must have decent sex lives, since they have plenty of children.

My view was put into perspective by a young Orthodox married couple selling real estate. I told them that I date plenty of women and have an active social life. Some women accept my advances and others decline. I bragged that, "My closing ratio is fifty percent." Many people are impressed by that statistic. The wife's response was jolting and accurate. "Eric, you are not married. Your closing ratio is zero."

The truth stings, but it needed to be said. Religious married people lead happier, healthier lives than those who jump from partner to partner having premarital sex.

What I have actually done and the number of people I have allegedly done it with are not pieces of information requiring disclosure. It adds nothing to the discussion and may cause my parents to use this book for more than balancing their uneven coffee table. A *klop on keppy* is quite painful.

One incident does need to be discussed, with the name left out to protect the guilty.

The biggest Jewish party night of the year is December 24. While Christians are celebrating their holy day, single Jews are out looking to meet each other at elaborate and sometimes expensive dances. The only things for Jews to do on December 24 and 25 when I was growing up were eat Chinese food, watch movies, and go bowling. Then some Jewish entrepreneurs came up with the idea of hosting Jewish singles events on December 24. Although some of them were given corny names such as the *Matzo Ball*, *Bagel Ball* and *Schmoozapalooza*,[43] the turnout showed that these events worked.

I took a mercenary approach to these events. The goal was to meet as many women as possible in one night. Collect several phone numbers. Assume some of the women were flaky and gave out their number despite not being interested. Take the interested women on dates. A man could spend the entire night talking to one woman, but that strategy is risky. If the situation does not work out, the man has spent money and time attending an event while ignoring plenty of available singles. If a guy meets a great girl at these parties, get her number and call her.

On more than one occasion (twice, to be exact), I instantly clicked with a woman within moments of entering the dance club. In both cases, my December 24 was spent engaging in some pretty passionate moments. In one of those two cases, we probably crossed the line and made a spectacle of ourselves in the club.

In one case my friends saw me with this girl draped all over me. I looked at them and mouthed the words, "I have no idea how to explain this." They laughed. The other case was stranger. She had known me for some time. At this December 24 dance, out of nowhere, she just groped me. I turned around, saw her, and the next thing I know we are in a semi-quiet part of the club engaging in behavior that is not appropriate for a public place.

If this woman was my future wife, perhaps all could be forgiven. The problem is we both knew that we were wrong for each other. Lust took over. Men who saw me smiled and gave signs of approval. "You're the man" was said more than once. Whenever a guy is dancing suggestively with a girl on the dance floor, he becomes the envy of other guys. Every guy wants to be the coolest guy in the room. On this night, I was. I had no business being with a woman that hot engaging in such salaciousness.

The problem is that while I enjoyed several hours of physical contact, I completely ignored the purpose of attending the December 24 Jewish dance. There were plenty of eligible single women there, many of whom could have possibly been my future wife. If I run into them at another event, they may look at me in disgust as the guy behaving badly at a party. Hopefully they saw nothing, but that concern would be nonexistent had I spent the evening thinking with the brain above my trousers.

While I succeeded in having a passionate night with a gorgeous Jewish woman, I totally failed in my quest to meet a potential Jewish wife.

When it comes to lust, I should change my name from Eric to Erij, an acronym I invented that from now on forever stands for Error in Judgment. At least the women at these dances are Jewish.

The mechitza separates the Jewish men from the Jewish women. There is no mechitza to separate Jews from non-Jews. In the Orthodox world, total separation is the only solution.

This is not bigotry. I have a deep respect for Christianity. It is a beautiful religion with lovely traditions I know nothing about. It will never be in my home. My home will be a Jewish home with Jewish traditions.

For those who want to avoid intermarrying, do not even date outside the faith. On more than one occasion I dated a woman who promised to convert to Judaism. These women were not liars. They meant it when they said it. They just did not realize the pull their own faith would have when it mattered most. Even people who are not religious will often turn to their religion during a crisis. When a relative is near death or even ill, a natural response for a Christian is to pray to their God in the church they know.

In one case the woman told me upfront that she would never convert away from Catholicism. We should have stayed far away from each other. Instead we spent six months together. When the inevitable breakup happened, it was a volatile conversation that measured high on the Richter scale. There was acrimony and blame. While we both said at one point we would always be friends, the truth is we will probably never speak to each other again. Being in a room with her brings back the anger. This is what often happens when people put short-term pleasure above long-term love.

Judaism has built-in bulwarks to prevent these very mistakes. This Jewish boy knows that the right thing to do is stay on his own side of the mechitza for his own good. A police officer does not patrol a dangerous neighborhood without his protective armor. The mechitza protects Jewish people from letting biological urges that Hashem instilled in all of us overwhelm what Hashem intended for his people.

Chapter 9: Sports Lunacy: My career as a Jewish football player

I feel bad for Christians. No God should be so cruel as to schedule the holy day in conflict with the National Football League. Growing up before the age of cellphones and Internet access was agony on my Christian friends who had to sit through a Sunday sermon when they wanted to be watching pro football.

The Jewish Sabbath conflicts with college football, but that was not a concern for me. Growing up, Saturday was about going to synagogue and then doing my homework. Either the homework got done or I could not watch football on Sunday. Attending the University of Judaism is not the way to pursue a football career. At best we may have produced a team accountant or surgeon.

We all have our religious devotion tested. For non-Orthodox Jews, seemingly easy choices can be agonizing. My burning passion has always been football. My Judaism has been tested most when it conflicted with football.

Hashem would be watching football too if he did not already know the score

An old joke about God asks that if he is so powerful, can he make a rock so big that even he can't lift it? I wonder if the God who created football can create a game where even he would not know the score. Creating the world is hard work. God rested on the seventh day. Shouldn't his work have been rewarded with a cold beverage and a good football game? What is the point of being God if even simple pleasures get ruined? Perhaps the score of the game is not pre-ordained. The players have free will. The choices they make determine who wins. God should be powerful enough to avoid running into anyone or anything that should reveal the score to him before he has a chance to watch the game himself. A few threats of lightning bolts should deter people from purposely leaking the information.

Even if God were able to somehow not know everything all the time, he would still unfortunately not have time to watch football. He is kind of busy helping seven billion people not blow up the world he created. American workers get two weeks of paid vacation. God does not have that luxury and I do not think he is financially compensated despite working harder than everybody else.

Let's get the obvious complaint from others out of the way at the start. Plenty of people have zero interest in football. My response is that these people including my parents have a right to exist. I have a right to not understand them.

Most children learn about sports from their parents. I did not have that (some would say mis) fortune. The Oakland Raiders won the Super Bowl on my fifth birthday. I had no idea what football was, but I thought the Raiders logo was the coolest thing I had ever seen. My favorite color was black. Their logo of the pirate with the eye patch over one eye was marketing at its very best.

A couple months before I turned nine, my next-door neighbor took me to my first football game. I was instantly hooked and began collecting football cards. Although collecting cards lasted only a few weeks, my love for the game lasted forever. I sat down and watched my first football game on television in what turned out to be the last week of the 1980 season. The Raiders won that game. I watched all of their playoff games. My bedtime caused me to miss the end of the games, but they won them. Shortly after I turned nine, they won the Super Bowl again. I was a Raider for life. A few days after I turned twelve, they won another Super Bowl. They have not won since, but being Jewish prepared me for plenty of frustration.

The Jews are the world's outcasts. There are so few of us, but we prosper against all odds. At least one billion of the planet's seven billion people dislike if not outright hate us. It is us against the world and we are still here.

The Raiders were the outlaws of the NFL. They were hated, and wore that hatred as a badge of honor. When they won the Super Bowl, it was sheer joy watching the rest of the league fume. Raiders owner Al Davis was a Brooklyn Jew and a rebel to his core. His mantra was "Just win, baby!"[44]

Davis's critics saw him as a soulless Machiavellian who believed that the ends justified the means. The Raiders were known for cheating and playing dirty. The Raiders had two rules on the blackboard in the locker room. Players were to show up on Sunday and stay out of trouble with the law. At the bottom of the blackboard a note read that if you obeyed rule number one, you could ignore rule number two. Davis often provided the bail money.[45]

This provides an incomplete picture of Al Davis and the Raiders. The other side of the coin is that the Raiders were a home for players who had been rejected from other teams for not fitting in. Being a misfit was the norm on the Raiders. The Jews were rejected other people. So were the Raiders. If you were a good player, Al Davis would make room for you. If you were a Raider, you were a Raider for life. Like Judaism, Raiders did not convert away from the Silver and Black.

As a Jew, Davis knew what it was like to face discrimination. Known in the media mainly for his misdeeds, Davis practiced Tikkun Olam in his own way. He hired the first black NFL head coach of the modern era and the first Hispanic NFL head coach. He hired the first female NFL executive, an accomplished Jewish attorney named Amy Trask.[46] Davis trusted his wife and virtually nobody else, but he trusted Trask. She worked for Davis until his death on Yom Kippur of 2012. As a young boy I saw being a Jew and being a Raider as a perfect synthesis.

The only thing better than watching football was playing football. I hated snow, but I loved playing snow football. We would play in the streets until dark, stopping only for the occasional car. Although we wore gloves in the cold, I found that gloves made it tougher to catch the ball. When my gloves ripped, I would leave them ripped. I made some great catches with ripped gloves.

To a Jewish mother, ripped gloves are not acceptable. My mother bought me several pairs, and they all got ripped. She stopped buying them out of frustration, but then her worst nightmare came true. Perhaps the neighbors thought we were poor. More likely they were just being nice. One December I received five or six pairs of gloves as Hanukkah and Christmas presents from my neighbors. My mom was mortified that the neighborhood was providing clothing for her child. She did not need to worry. I ended up ripping all of those gloves as well. Neither she nor the neighbors ever bought me another pair again.

I remember being about nine when I came inside from playing football in the street. I was every color of the rainbow. There was red blood, green grass stains, brown mud, black coal markings, and whitish silver ice. Some of the kids had yellow, but that was never to be discussed anywhere. Thankfully I was not one of those kids. I came in the house triumphantly, having scored the winning touchdown. I spiked the football and did my end zone touchdown dance celebration learned from Billy "White Shoes" Johnson.[47] He remains the greatest dancer in the history of football.

Winning touchdowns are less important to my mother than disgusting messes being tracked into the house. What Jewish mom cares more about a clean floor than in nurturing football greatness? Apparently many Jewish moms shared my mother's affliction.

My father had a different take. He sat me down on the toilet as he applied Mercurochrome and Iodine to my wounds. Winning touchdowns did not impress him either.

"Son, are you getting paid for this?"

One day I was sure I would be, but at age nine I was not.

"Do you have any endorsement deals?"

I had no idea what he was talking about.

"Are you selling sneakers or on a box of Wheaties?"

Again, that would come in good time.

"Son, let me you give you some advice. The next time eleven people are coming at you ready to kill you, give them the d@mn ball."

Protesting was a waste of time.

"Look Eric, it's not personal. They do not hate you. Well, maybe some of them hate your guts, but that's not the point. If you were not holding the football, they would not try to tackle you. Also, there are two end zones. A guy who runs into a brick wall of eleven people deserves to get bruised. Run toward the other goal where nobody is trying to stop you."

He knew full well that would mean a score for the other team. Frustration only deepened when my mom joined the conversation.

"Honey, why can't you kids all just share the ball?"

There comes a time when a child wants to scream, "You just don't get it." Those kids get grounded. I knew better for once. Mom continued.

"Better yet Eric, why doesn't every kid bring a ball? Then they will all have a ball they can play with."

For the love of all things holy, this was not a white elephant gift exchange where everybody is supposed to end up happy! Football is a brutal, violent game where some people win and some people lose. Players sacrifice their bodies for glory. The lucky few make millions of dollars doing it.

My own football career did not developed as I had hoped. I could claim my parents wrecked my football career but reality would tell a different story. I grew up to be only five feet, five inches tall and weigh 128 pounds according to my driver's license. As a kid I was always the littlest. Thankfully my competitive spirit frequently allowed me to avoid the ignominy of suffering from being the last kid picked. Running fast and being able to catch the ball helped matters. It is tough to hit a guy who cannot be caught.

While being a football player was not in the cards, I could still be part of an NFL team. Like any Jewish boy, I could be the team doctor for the Raiders. That plan went out the window when I realized I hated the sight of blood, especially my own. I also hate needles. I could have been the team accountant except that I did not fit the stereotype of a boring technocrat. While I happen to know at least one CPA who is a fun guy, too many Jewish accountants are grouchy individuals who prefer numbers on spreadsheets to people. My own football career would plateau at being a fan watching on television. This is where Judaism became an issue.

For many Jewish football fans, college football matters. The games are almost always on Shabbos. The Iron Bowl is a big deal in Alabama. When bitter rivals at the universities of Alabama and Auburn play each other, everything stops in the entire state except Shabbos. One synagogue in Birmingham, Alabama had an enterprising idea how to incorporate the game into the community. The rabbi confiscated the cellphones of all congregants. People are not supposed to use cellphones on Shabbos, but this game was too serious to allow temptation into the equation. After a lovely community day with the afternoon Minchah and evening Maariv services completed, it was time to end the Sabbath. Once the Havdalah ritual brought Shabbos to a close, the congregation watched the game together as a Jewish football family.[48] Cellphones were returned once the game ended.

I rarely had this conflict. My interest is Sunday professional football. Many of my Christian friends prayed that Homer Simpson's clergyman Reverend Lovejoy or his clone would just shut up and be done with the service before kickoff. East Coast people were usually in good shape because the games did not start until 1:00 p.m. Those on the West Coast where games started at 10:00 a.m. had no chance. For most of the year, NFL games are on Sunday. To create more excitement, the league put games on Saturday and Sunday during the last two weeks of the regular season. The first two weeks of the playoffs always have games on Saturday and Sunday. This is before getting to games that fall on Yontiffs and other serious days on the Jewish calendar.

It is one thing to wait three or four hours. Waiting twenty-four hours is much tougher. My junior year in college saw the Raiders play at their archrival Kansas City Chiefs on Monday Night Football. That game was on Yom Kippur. I waited twenty-four hours and avoided newspapers. This was 1992, before the Internet age. I even avoided most of my male friends. I especially avoided a couple of male enemies just in case they decided to purposely reveal the score. This was at the University of Judaism, where they should not have been watching the game anyway.

After twenty-four hours, I prepared to sit down on Tuesday night to watch the game. On my way to the lounge to pop the tape somebody made for me into the VCR, I ran into my friend Elana. Sexism on my part had me figuring there was no way a girl would know anything about football. I said hello and goodbye. Before I could leave, she said, "Your Raiders sucked last night." She turned ashen when I looked at her and said, "I...taped...the...game." I chased her up and down several flights of stairs. I would have let her live had I caught up to her, but she smartly took no chances.

No good deed goes unpunished. Doing right did not work. Unlike a regular television show, live sporting events have to be watched live. Violating the spirit of the law would be the order of the day going forward as long as the bare letter of Jewish law was obeyed.

Yom Kippur in 2002 began on a Sunday night. Most football games on the West Coast were done before sundown except for the night game. Naturally the Raiders were playing in the night game. It was a big road game at the hated Pittsburgh Steelers. Yom Kippur would begin around halftime.

My friend Eric and I made our decision. The television was turned on before sundown. Since Yom Kippur is the day of fasting for over twenty-four hours, a pair of Erics stuffed their faces full of burgers before the sun went down. A boring game meant we could head to synagogue sooner. The game was a thriller. The Raiders led 20-17 in the second half. Since our food was already consumed and the television was already on, we kept watching. We were not operating any electricity. The Raiders won 30-17 and we then high-tailed it to synagogue quite late. My friends knew exactly why I missed the beginning of the service. A holiday where Jews are supposed to atone for their sins saw me rack up one more transgression just as the holiday was beginning.

This may seem like a trivial dilemma for some, but the NFL takes it seriously. New York has the largest Jewish population in the United States. When the New York Giants were scheduled one year to play on Yom Kippur, the league switched the day of the game. Another year the season, which now traditionally begins on a Thursday night, conflicted with Rosh Hashanah. While the league cannot alter games every week, the very first week of the season is special. The league moved the inaugural kickoff game from Thursday to Wednesday.[49]

ESPN uber-announcer Chris Berman is Jewish. From 1987 through 2006 he hosted the highlights show *NFL Primetime*.[50] He would throw in Jewish humor that had nothing to do with the games. Several non-Jewish players had last names that sounded Jewish. When showing plays featuring Bernie Parmalee, Rod Bernstein and Steve Israel, Berman would speak in a fake Yiddish accent. When a player named Elijah was running for a touchdown, Berman referenced a Passover ritual by thundering that Elijah had the cup of wine and the football.[51] Just like that, Elijah was gone! Touchdown!

Berman's best moment along this line came when I was in college. He started out with his usual, "Welcome to *NFL Primetime*!" He then surprised my friends and I watching the program by saying, "We would like to wish the Jewish members of our audience a happy Rosh Hashanah!" He added in one more line. "For those of you watching this broadcast on the East Coast, you should be in temple right now."[52] He waved his finger and said, "We caught you." My friends looked at each other in stunned disbelief and then relief. We were on the West Coast. The sun had yet to go down. This time we raced to temple out of excitement that an ESPN broadcaster took time from football highlights to spread joy to his fellow Jewish football fans.

This is bigger than football. For many non-Orthodox American Jews, balancing Jewish law with American culture is a struggle. The Orthodox to their credit always put Jewish law first. The rest of us truly wrestle with American traditions such as football on Shabbos, Halloween and the level of kosher-style we can live with observing.

One rabbinical student in the early 1990s is now a rabbi in Detroit. He is also a die-hard Detroit Lions fan. His idea was to hide a small television set below where the rabbi leads the service. It would look like he was bowing to pray when in reality he would be checking the score during the service. He was only kidding, and I am pretty sure the rest of the rabbis at that temple would disallow such expenditures.

I knew by 2008 that my football obsession was life-long based on a pair of trips that elicited different reactions. In the summer of 2008 I visited Israel for the first time. I was hoping to come back with a changed perspective and have all of life's answers revealed. It was a fun trip. I had a nice time. I prayed at the Wall. Except for more (still icky) Hummus, it was similar to my 2003 trip to Singapore. Both were pleasant trips that provided lifelong memories. Because I grew up knowing about the Holocaust, the Yad Vashem Holocaust Memorial made me angry, not teary-eyed.

Neither Israel nor Singapore affected me like my 2006 trip to Canton, Ohio. Canton is the holy birthplace of professional football and the home of the Pro Football Hall of Fame. As soon as I touched down on that hallowed ground I felt something powerful. When I got inside and saw the exhibits, I cried my eyes out. There were men of all races and ethnicities crying as they explained to their children the significance of the moment. I have not been back to Israel yet, but I have returned to Canton a couple more times. This is not to denigrate Israel. When I want to feel a powerful emotional Jewish connection, I go to Brooklyn. Coney Island is my Jerusalem. Coney Island even rivals Canton.

In addition to playing football and watching football, there is still a way for young Jews to be gridiron heroes. My friends and I were masters at football video games. Former Raiders coach and legendary NFL announcer

John Madden created the greatest video football game in history. Legions of football fans have been playing *Madden Football*[53] for over twenty-five years. In 1990, the world of Judaism again threatened to interrupt the life and death matter of football that consumed a pair of freshmen friends.

I could beat the computer by myself. Jason could beat the computer by himself. Put us on the same team, and we would lose. Jason insisted that my video quarterback threw the ball badly, but the truth is he was a lousy offensive lineman. The only thing he successfully blocked was the television in case somebody else tried to interrupt our game. Jason disputes my version of events. He can write his own book.

One Friday evening just before sundown, Jason and I were engrossed in *Madden Football* when a fellow freshman entered the room. She was a Catholic in the process of converting to Judaism. Her reform conversion was complete but she felt a conservative conversion would give her more legitimacy. She wanted us to go to synagogue because she was performing some conversion ritual. She may not have been doing that. We were not exactly listening. We had a game to win. When we told her we were busy, she was incredulous.

"You are not just obsessed over a game. You are obsessed over a game of a game."

I may have mentioned something about recommending she save her voice for temple by staying quiet while we were playing. She threw down her books and let loose a tirade.

"This is totally unfair. I have to read all of these books, take all of these classes, and obey all of these laws so that I can convert to a religion where guys like you never read the books, take none of the classes, and don't obey any of the laws. Yet you guys are considered more Jewish than me because of purity of bloodlines!"

The proper thing to do would be to explain to her that we would be equally Jewish when her conversion was complete. Judaism has no such thing as converts. There are Jews and non-Jews. Once somebody completes the conversion process, they are just as Jewish as someone born into the faith. Orthodox Jews require an Orthodox conversion, which is a much more arduous process. The idea of embracing all Jews regardless of bloodlines is the same. Perhaps the way I explained this to her was lost in translation. For some reason my response did not please her.

"Yeah, it's a real (bummer) isn't it?"

The actual word I used rhymed with witch. The next few seconds were a blur as a book flew past us and nearly damaged our faces. Video games teach men to duck and cover, athletes that we are. She stormed out of the room. For a girl not yet Jewish, her Catholic upbringing sure prepared her to apply the thick guilt trips.

"Jason, is this going to be one of those times where we do the right thing whether we want to or not?"

It was. At least Hashem invented the pause button. Jason left a note on the television reading, "Video game in progress. Do not turn off on pain of death." The girl was glad when we showed up to services. When the service ended, Jason and I showed our athletic ability by racing back to the dormitory lounge to make sure nobody had messed with the television. We saved a Jewish soul from leaving the faith and a football game from prematurely ending. Jewish and football history were both preserved. Video football is in my past due to time constraints, but my ability to start, stop and pause games whenever I wanted ended that ethical dilemma. Football games on television remained an agonizing issue.

One year Rosh Hashanah fell on Sunday, preventing me from turning on the television the entire day. My football obsession has me checking the NFL schedule the moment it comes out in April. This gives me five months to prepare a strategy for this very scenario. I remembered that the local Chabad House in Los Angeles near UCLA was down the block from what was then Maloney's (now O'Hara's) Sports Bar. I read exactly what times the games were on and estimated what time the services would be.

That day I bounced back and forth between the two locations. At the Chabad House, I wore traditional Jewish garb. At the sports bar I switched to my football clothing of a Raiders shirt and matching baseball cap. I kept dressing and undressing like Robin Williams in *Mrs. Doubtfire*. [54] I eventually got confused, forgot where I was, and showed up in my synagogue clothing at the sports bar. One definitely non-Jewish guy in the sports bar seemed confused when I asked him, "When is Minchah?" He had no idea what Minchah was but he let me know kickoff was in a few minutes. It could have been worse. I could have asked the rabbi when kickoff was. It didn't matter. In shul I was ignoring the service and thinking about the game. In the sports bar I was worried I was missing the service. At that moment I realized it was time to stop kidding myself.

The answer for people like me is to maintain integrity. Make a decision, be honest with myself about what I am doing, and do not make excuses or rationalizations. The decision should be made privately. There is no need to discuss it publicly unless one truly wants advice they plan to heed. Rosh Hashanah 2015 will be year 5776 for Jews. It runs from Sunday night through Tuesday night, encompassing Sunday Night Football and Monday Night Football. That is the opening week of the 2015 NFL season.

I will be watching football during the day on Sunday since the holiday will not start until later that night. I will be in synagogue Sunday night. The question will be whether to skip Sunday Night Football or leave the television on and arrive late to temple. That decision will be between Hashem and me. I will make an effort to obey the spirit as well as the letter of his laws. If I fail it will be because of my own shortcomings. I will make no excuses and accept the consequences of whatever decision I make. I love Judaism. I love football. We shall see.

Chapter 10: Dancing Lunacy: Nobody parties like a sharp dressed Chabad Rabbi

Rapper and actor Will Smith sang about the "Men in Black: Galaxy Defenders."[55] Even people who know nothing about Judaism have seen the men in black hats. They are the Judaic defenders. These people who look like a cross between the Amish and ZZ Top are from Chabad, Chasidic Jews who follow the teachings of the Lubavitcher Rebbe Menachem Schneerson. These are the Duck Dynasty rabbis. Their large hearts and devotion to preserving Judaism match their large beards. The Taliban stole the bearded look from Chasidic Jews and thankfully failed to give elongated whiskers a bad name. Unlike the Taliban, Chabad rabbis do not shoot somebody for trying to enjoy a L'Chaim with Schnapps. If you can't beat them, join them. The Taliban beat drinkers. Chabadniks join them.

Although I am not a member of the Chabad sect, I honor and respect this great organization. Many people see Chabadniks as people who stay in a room all day studying Torah, as if there is something wrong with that. These men work hard and study hard, but they also play hard within the rules of Judaism. They are serious about following Hashem's laws, but they also constantly preach that Hashem wants us to be joyful. Our lives should be filled with Simchah, the Hebrew word for joy. We even have a holiday called Simchas Torah, the joy of Torah.[56]

So many Chabad rabbis have brought joy to my life. Thanking them all is the least I can do. Anyone who thinks religious Jews are stuffy should dispel that notion now. Nobody, and I mean nobody, parties like an Orthodox Chabad rabbi.

Who is that Amish guy and why is he wearing the Rabbi's pants?

Jews are often seen as overly serious. We are studious. Many of our holidays are somber. Rosh Hashanah and Yom Kippur are about self-improvement. Passover tells the story of overcoming persecution. Most of Jewish history has been a struggle for survival.

This is not the complete story of Judaism, its holidays or its people. Hanukkah involves eight days of partying. Irish Catholics have one drinking holiday, St. Patrick's Day. Jews have two drinking holidays. Purim usually occurs around St. Patrick's Day. Simchas Torah is usually celebrated in September. Islam bans the consumption of alcohol, but alcohol is steeped in Jewish tradition. On Purim, Jews are told to drink until they cannot tell the difference between Mordechai and Esther.[57] This naturally leads the concept of "Eat, drink and be merry" to become "Drink, get drunk and fall down."

I have never been a drinker. My father left the liquor cabinet unlocked, which made alcohol boring. It was always available so I never wanted it. When people find out I do not drink, they ask me if I am in the twelve-step program. It is a sad commentary that people who do not drink alcohol are considered weird. I simply dislike the taste. Wine is overpriced bilgewater. I prefer soda. Dr. Brown's Black Cherry Soda is the greatest beverage on the planet. Plus it is kosher, even on Passover. As a non-drinker, it would be hypocritical of me to suddenly become religious on Purim and Simchas Torah. It is unseemly to claim Hashem's name to justify getting drunk.

Orthodox Jews devoting their lives to all 613 mitzvahs[58] get a pass. True believers can justify getting inebriated on Purim and Simchas Torah. My friend Greg is a true believer. One Simchas Torah I heard him yell, "Another beer for the boys of Torah!" I knew Greg had consumed enough alcohol when he shouted in shul, "Who is that Amish guy, and why is he wearing the rabbi's pants?"

Most of the room was drunk. There was only amusement, not embarrassment. I was the goalie. When my Jewish friends spilled out into the street, I gently kicked them back into the shul to keep them from getting run over by traffic. Eventually the local Chabad got police permission to seal off the street in front of the Chabad House for a couple of hours so the party could stretch down the block.

Most Jews learn as children about the miracle of oil that gave us Hanukkah. I was one of very few people who personally witnessed the miracle of alcohol that gave two enterprising young Chabadniks a Hanukkah menorah.

The last night of Hanukkah was maybe an hour away and these two guys at the Chabad House could not find their menorah to light candles. How does somebody in a Chabad House not find a menorah? That question was never answered. They had their menorah the first seven nights. How does one lose a menorah that just sits there? That question also remained unanswered. One of the guys was named Wheels. By the end of the night he would be off his wheels. He and his friend never found a menorah, but he did find several bottles of beer. He and his friend quickly downed eight bottles of beer between them. The last thing people should do after consuming that much beer is play with matches. They had the idea to stick a candle in each bottle, using candle wax to fuse the bottles together. They made a menorah out of beer bottles.

A menorah actually holds nine candles, not eight. Eight candles represent the eight nights of Hanukkah. One candle known as the shamash stands taller above the other candles in the same way the king on a chessboard is taller than the pawns. Because Wheels needed a shamash larger than the other beer bottles, he and his friend soon downed a bottle of "Rabbi Smirnoff." I have no idea how two guys can consume eight bottles of beer and one bottle of Russian vodka and remember the prayers, but they did. They then spent the night dancing on the tables, which has less to do with Judaism than inebriation.

One of the great Chabad rabbis is Rabbi Shlomo Cunin. From his Los Angeles office, he has run Chabad of the West Coast for decades. Many of his thirteen children spread the Rebbe's message from Chabad Houses up and down Los Angeles and surrounding areas.

He is the main rabbi seen dancing on the annual Chabad telethon. How a man over sixty-five can dance for seven hours is beyond me. I get tired after seven hours of football, and I am only watching. Incidentally, the Chabad telethon usually coincides with the first NFL Sunday. On the West Coast, the telethon starts after all the afternoon games have ended. Football fans have no excuses to miss it. A non-Jewish friend of mine from India observed the telethon once. He remarked, "Eric, I know nothing about your religion, but that telethon guy sure knows how to party."

When Rabbi Cunin needed more Jews to attend Shabbos services, he went to the local Jewish fraternity house of AEPi. Some prayers such as the Mourner's Kaddish require a Minyan, ten males over the age of thirteen. Without this threshold, those prayers cannot be said. Cunin made a bet with the frat boys. If he could out-drink them, they had to show up the next day. When asked which frat boy he wanted to face off against, he replied, "All of you." An hour later a dozen frat boys were passed out on the floor. The big, burly Russian rabbi was still dancing. The frat boys kept their word. The frat boys now warn each other on the rare occasions he passes by the frat house. His legend has been passed down like Will Ferrell's "Frank the Tank" in *Old School*.[59] Don't mess with this rabbi. He knows how to party.

He also knows when to party and when to get serious. The leader of this entire movement has to balance business, politics, social media and a myriad of other skills while maintaining the unique religious Jewish essence that is Chabad. He has said on more than one occasion that, "There is no such thing as an atheist on a turbulent plane or in a bear market."

While Chabad itself is steeped in Chasidic Judaism, it helps people of all faiths. Chabad of the West Coast runs drug treatment centers that have gotten many people off of the scourge of drugs. Many Hollywood celebrities over the years have embraced Chabad. Some of them like Billy Crystal are Jewish. Many of them are not. When the late Robin Williams grew a beard, he joked that he was auditioning to be part of the Chabad telethon.[60] Christian actor Jon Voight has been a major supporter of Chabad.[61]

Chabad was in financial trouble a long time ago. They owed money to a Mexican business and the Mexican company was threatening to call in the loan. The story relayed to me was that Rabbi Cunin promised to pay back all of the money but needed more time. The Mexican business played hardball and told Cunin that he was to immediately give them "all or nothing."

In the courtroom, Cunin remembered that the Lubavitcher Rebbe commanded that we should always be happy. Be joyful.[62] Do not let the pressures of life cause depression. During a courtroom break, Cunin heeded the Rebbe's words and started dancing in celebration in the courthouse hallway. Some attendees thought he had lost his mind, dancing right before a case that could be decided against him.

While this was going on, Jewish United States Senator Rudy Boschwitz was on the phone with the Mexican government. Boschwitz's message was clear. Mexico owed the United States significantly more money that this one Chabad House owed this one business. If this Mexican business called in its loan of the Chabad House, the United States would call in its entire loan to the whole nation of Mexico.

The Mexican government quickly contacted the company just before court was about to resume. In a panic, the company approached Cunin and agreed to work out an installment plan. Cunin insisted that he was an honest man, and that the business would eventually get every penny owed to them. Until then, Cunin reminded them that they gave him an earlier ultimatum. "You said all or nothing. One day you will get it all. For now, you get nothing!"

That Friday night Shabbos was especially sweet, a victory celebration. Cunin even walked past the AEPi frat house to invite them. Some of the frat boys hid. Others just quickly agreed to join him. None of them openly opposed him. They knew not to mess with Rabbi Shlomo Cunin.

One time when I was walking along busy Wilshire Blvd. near my home, a big van came near me from across the street. It did a quick U-turn, burned rubber, and came to a screeching halt right in front of me. My good neighborhood was not known for drive-by shootings. This was a different kind of drive-by. A booming voice called out, "Did you put on tefillin today?"

Caught off guard, I told Rabbi Cunin that I had not. He responded, "Good. I have some in my car." Rabbi Cunin does not ask questions. It was understood I was going to do it, especially since there was not a single valid reason to refuse. As he was wrapping my arm to fulfill the ritual, he remarked, "Remember, you are holding up traffic on Wilshire Blvd. You have to do this quickly." Only then did I notice that we were not on the sidewalk, but in the right lane of oncoming traffic. After we completed the ritual and got on the sidewalk, I complimented him for his inspiring Yom Kippur remarks a few weeks earlier. I told him that his speech would have a shelf life of 1,000 years. He responded, "Just make sure not to leave it on the shelf."

I once told him that while I thought he was controversial, I respected him. He replied that, "People are only controversial after they are dead."

His sons Chaim and Mendy are about my age, so confiding in and learning from them has always been comfortable. Their wives Tova and Rivkah have invited me to their homes many times. Better cooks may exist somewhere I have never been.

I have met many Chabad rabbis through Chaim and Mendy. Their father is known worldwide, but I refuse to make false claims for personal gain. When they ask if I know the father, I always say the same thing. "I am dear friends with Chaim and Mendy but I will never claim a friendship with their father for one reason. Friendship implies equality. Cunin Sr. and I are not equals. He is way up there. I am down here." They understand.

It is the same attitude I have toward Rabbi David Wolpe. He is not that much older than me, but everybody should have a few people that bring about an instant internal humility. I could become a billionaire, a scholar, or some other powerful man and one thing will not change. Wolpe will always be the teacher and I will always be the student. That is just the way it is and should be.

Rabbi Cunin has taught many people. I am just one of them. I have much more to learn, and Mendy and Chaim are always there to offer advice when it is sought. In addition to them and my childhood Chabad rabbis, many other emissaries of the Rebbe have made me feel welcome all over the world.

In 2003 I visited Singapore on a business trip. Rabbi Mordechai Abergel heads up a community of Asian Jews more than 1,000 strong that goes back generations.[63] I celebrated Purim with them, and 250 Jews turned out. When twenty-five percent of any community turns out for one event, that community has a great leader.

In 2013 I was in the hotbed of Judaism: North Dakota. I went on J-Date and was curious how many profiles would show up. In Los Angeles men sift through hundreds of profiles. In North Dakota there were exactly three. None were Jewish. They just liked Jewish guys. This concluded Jewish dating in North Dakota. Nevertheless, I did make a new friend. Rabbi Yonah Grossman heads up Chabad of Fargo. If there is one Jew anywhere, Chabad will find them and reach out to them. There have to be Jews in North Dakota. Rabbi Grossman will find them all.

In August of 2014, Rabbi Yisroel Hahn of Spokane, Washington taught me a fun song during a Friday night Shabbos dinner.

"Young folks, old folks, everybody come.

Come to our Chabad House, we'll have a lot of fun.

Kiss the Mezuzah you'll find hanging on the door.

We'll have fun learning Torah like we've never learned before."[64]

That song has been stuck in my head for several months. Now it is stuck in yours.

Rabbi Yisroel Shmotkin of Milwaukee, Wisconsin is one of the kindest and most disciplined men I have ever met. His daily Shachris services begin precisely at 7:00 a.m. I stayed at his Chabad House for a few days. There was no way I would do this without contributing to the morning Minyan. Early mornings were agony for a fellow who never broke the college habit of being a night person. One of the young Chabadniks would wake me up at 6:50 a.m. We would put on clothing from the night before, brush our teeth, and stagger downstairs. After the service we would stagger back upstairs and return to bed. The only other person I knew who prayed that early in the morning was my dad's father. He had an excuse. He went to bed at 7:30 p.m. at night.

Rabbi Dov Wagner heads up the Chabad House at the University of Southern California. Being a college campus rabbi is more difficult than being the rabbi in a regular community. A campus rabbi has to relate to the students and help them go down the right path with a gentle and skilled touch. Too much pressure could push them away from Judaism permanently, which almost happened to me due to the UJ.

A campus Chabad rabbi has to show the joy of Judaism without compromising on the strict doctrines passed down from the Rebbe. Reform Jewish synagogues can be more flexible in appealing to students up to a certain point. Orthodox shuls do not have this luxury. USC Chabad is thriving because Dov and his wife Runya infuse school spirit into their programming. A particularly enjoyable Shabbos evening featured Alan "Shlomo" Veingrad, the only Orthodox Jewish football player to have won a Super Bowl ring.[65] His lecture was fifty percent football, fifty percent Torah, and one hundred percent meaningful.

USC's rival school is UCLA. The University of California Los Angeles is well represented by Orthodox Hillel Rabbi Aryeh Kaplan and his wife Sharona as well as Chabad Rabbi and Rebbetzin Dovid and Elisa Gurevich. Three other Chabad rabbis also played a major role in the next phase of my career development. They may refuse to accept the credit, but I am giving it to them anyway. This development is happening right now.

Chapter 11: Philosophical Lunacy: When is a speech not a speech?

Forget non-controversial issues like abortion and gay rights. The most controversial issue is speech. The First Amendment prevents the government from imposing some limits on our freedom of speech. The First Amendment does not apply to parents, who can tell their children to sit down, be quiet, and stop talking for as long as the parents want. The Fifth Amendment allows defendants to refuse to answer questions in a courtroom on the grounds that they may incriminate themselves. The Fifth Amendment does not provide any protections to children, who are forced to answer any and all questions their parents ask of them always. Children are often forced to speak when they wish to remain silent and remain silent when they wish to speak. This leaves one critical question.

When does speech go from being "speech" to being "a speech?" When does a speech begin? Is it when the speaker starts talking or when the audience starts listening? When does a speech end? Is it after the speaker finishes their prepared remarks? How does the question and answer session fit in? Most importantly, how can you be expected to know what I am talking about if I don't know what I am talking about?

6,000 years from now, rabbis may sit around the table and debate these very questions. More likely, they will probably debate RaMBaM and Rashi and ignore these questions completely. Either way, three Chabad rabbis, one Jewish activist, and one stunning Jewish brunette girl played a role in my becoming a Jewish speaker.

Entering the Jewish speaking circuit

After fifteen years, I left Wall Street in September of 2009 to become a full-time professional speaker. My exit from Wall Street had nothing to do with the 2008 financial crisis. I felt a calling. My speaking career started as a tiny joke. With hard work, it turned into an enormous one.

In 2007, a very attractive Jewish brunette told me to start a blog. I had absolutely no idea what a blog was. I just wanted to go out with her, so I told her, "Duh, ok." She could have told me to start a cult and I would have replied, "Duh, ok" without asking her what my cult would be. My dad's mother thought that you catch a cult when you don't feel well. Chicken soup, chicken cutlets and blintzes cure cults.

After agreeing to start a blog, this (still) technologically incompetent individual went online to find out what a blog was. I learned that a blog was an acronym for a weblog, also known as an online diary. I told the girl she was out of her mind. "Nobody will care what I have to say, nor should they. If I become an authority quoted on anything, America is lost." She then batted her eyelashes, so I started blogging.

My passions are politics and football, so I began covering politics during the week and football and other lighthearted interests on the weekend. I made two decisions early on. I was not going to talk about my friends, my family, or myself. I was not going to contribute to America becoming the nation of Narcissista. My goal was to convince people to think a certain way about ideas that mattered to me. My second rule was that I would establish myself as an opinion writer rather than an unbiased news source. Credibility matters to me. Whenever somebody would read my opinions and accuse me of being biased, I would respond that opinion writing by definition is biased. What mattered was if they could prove me wrong. If they did, I would comfortably admit that and be glad I learned something new. I would never demonize somebody personally just because they disagreed with me. I also banned commenters from using profanity or launching personal attacks. They could lambaste my ideas without getting in the gutter.

My blog debuted on March 11, 2007. Obsessed with performance metrics, I tracked my daily statistics. One day twelve people read me. Then fifteen. One day even twenty people read my column. I figured it was a friend of mine clicking on the link twenty times. Then one day I had over one hundred hits. Somebody in the blogosphere linked to my column and said that it contained some common sense ideas. I sent the Big Dog an online thank-you note for the link.

My parents taught me to avoid arrogance. I have never been comfortable bragging about myself. Unfortunately, getting people to read my blog required marketing. I went on other sites and told people to look at me. I still promote myself, and I still detest doing it.

Three months after my blog debuted, my friend Larry Greenfield invited me to be a panelist on a political panel at a meeting of Jewish political activists. *American Thinker* analysts Thomas Lifson and Richard Baehr brought sophisticated policy chops to the panel.[66] Larry moderated the panel, which he described as having, "bloggers, scholars and thinkers."

While I am capable of speaking seriously, my natural inclination toward being the wiseacre class clown never subsided. "So Larry says this panel contains bloggers, scholars and thinkers. Larry is a scholar. Richard and Tom work at *American Thinker*. I guess that makes me (sigh)…the blogger. See me after the panel Larry."

The crowd laughed. After fifteen minutes and sustained applause, Larry told me that, "A six-pointed star (of David) was born." People flooded my table wanting to shake my hand and take their picture with me. I was invited to sit at the head table. This was new to me and I loved every minute of it.

I answered a ton of questions. "How long have you been a speaker?" The truth was I had been a speaker for about fifteen minutes.

"Will you speak to our group?" Why not? Of course I would.

"Who is your agent?" Why would I have an agent? I am a stockbrokerage professional. I know nothing about the entertainment industry. Agents are for people who have people. Then somebody asked the question that changed my life.

"How much do you charge?"

The light bulb immediately went off. There was money to be made with this. I told people I work on a case-by-case basis, which was true since I did not have a single case yet. I decided to market myself as a political comedian because there were tons of political speakers willing to opine about anything and everything. Many of them were angry, boring or both. I wanted people to laugh and they wanted to laugh.

I gave a few local speeches around town but the money was very small. Some groups did not pay speakers at all. They gave the speaker a free meal and nothing more. Larry advised me to never speak for free. Even if groups only gave fifty dollars for gasoline, that separated me from people who spoke for free. Many groups could always find politicians willing to speak for free, but Larry was right. People are paid what they are worth. I began telling people that, "I believe in free speech, but I don't do it."[67]

I asked Larry how to make more money and he told me that most speakers earn income from book sales. I told Larry I did not have a book, so he told me to write one. I told him I didn't want to, and he reminded me that I would not make money. At that moment I said, "Great, now I'm an author." I wrote three political comedy books.

In September of 2009 I went on the speaking circuit full-time. In November of 2009 I gave my first major speech outside of California at a Texas convention. By 2010 I was traveling around the country giving speeches. Political groups were flying me out, paying me to speak, putting me up in nice hotels and private homes, and recommending me to other groups. I became a frequent radio guest of some large talk radio programs.

To my surprise, I noticed in 2012 that I had spoken in thirty-eight states. At that moment I realized that to speak in all fifty states was realistic. A free trip to Alaska allowed that one to come easily. I made five speeches in nine days during a Hawaii trip that featured plenty of paid vacation time. By early 2013, I had spoken in forty-six states. Only Vermont, Louisiana, North Dakota and Kansas remained. Knocking off those final four states became very difficult.

As a political speaker, Vermont and North Dakota were proving near impossible to penetrate. The two states could not be more different politically. Vermont is one of the most liberal states in America. They even have a proud socialist as their United States Senator. Bernie Sanders is Jewish and a hero on the left. North Dakota is very conservative. Both states are very small in terms of population. There are far fewer groups to speak to than in states like California and Texas.

Reaching out to political groups in Vermont was pointless. One guy laid out the problem for me. "Look, you seem like a nice guy, but we don't have political conversations in Vermont. Everybody agrees with each other. We are a one-party state. There is no dissent here. We all vote liberal. We don't need meetings, much less speakers."

A North Dakota politico offered a similar message for a different reason. "Eric, people go to meetings when they're upset. We're happy here. The oil boom has made us rich. Unemployment is at three percent. We all vote conservative and then go enjoy our lives. There is nothing to complain about. We don't need speakers. Our politicians stay out of the way and let things work."

I did manage to convince some young activists to put together a political comedy night in Fargo, North Dakota in June of 2013. By the time I arrived, North Dakota was state number forty-nine. The last holdout was Kansas. A political group invited me to speak in Hays, Kansas, halfway between Denver and Kansas City. On September 25, 2013, I gave that speech and could now claim I had spoken in all fifty states. Checking off states forty-seven and forty-eight was far tougher. Those speeches affected my Jewish life and my career.

Despite having an advanced degree, I was embarrassingly geographically challenged. Despite eighteen years in New York, I had no idea that New York shared a border with Vermont. How was this possible? New York was in the mid-Atlantic and Vermont was all the way in New England. I went to New York public schools my entire life, which is probably why I don't know anything. When I looked at the map and saw that New York bordered Vermont, I checked my calendar.

I was speaking on a Saturday night in April of 2013 to a political women's group in Albany. The New York state capital was right near the Vermont border. I had no speeches to give in Vermont, but at least I could set foot on Vermont soil. I could visit all fifty states even if I did not speak in them. It was something. Whenever I went to a place where I knew nobody, I reached out to the political community and the Jewish community. When I searched online, I noticed that the day after my Albany speech was Lag B'Omer. Chabad of Vermont was having a barbecue.

I called Rabbi Yitzchok Raskin and asked him for permission to come to the Lag B'Omer BBQ. He asked what I did professionally, as any rabbi normally would. I told him that I was a political speaker, but that I never bring my politics into the synagogue. My goal was to speak in all fifty states, but since nothing turned up in Vermont at least I could visit all fifty states and make lifelong friends. He asked me very simple questions that made me think deeper about what should have been painfully obvious.

"Do you only speak to political groups?"

At this point I had, but there was no reason it had to be that way. "Rabbi, I had a thought. Would it be ok if I spoke for five minutes at your barbecue? I would not discuss politics. I could tell Chabad-friendly stories about my Chabad experiences."

Rabbi Raskin was fine with the idea, but he asked me one other question. "Does that count?"

The answer was obvious. "You know, I actually don't know. I guess it counts. It has to count. I speak to people. This must count, otherwise you would not be considered people and you are definitely people."

He pointed out that the rules for my life were my own, but I still had to be honest with myself. I determined that as long as it was an actual speech, it would count. During the barbecue, I shared my Chabad stories and the twenty or thirty people at the barbecue laughed. It was a great Lag B'Omer, and Vermont was state forty-seven checked off.

Louisiana was far more nerve-wracking. I was only in town for twenty-four hours in May of 2013 to give one political speech on a Friday. My flight arrived Friday morning from Nashville, Tennessee. By Saturday I would be on my way back to Los Angeles. Several days before my event, it was canceled. Despite a successful appearance on the local political talk radio station in New Orleans, there were no political events occurring. After exhausting every political possibility, I reached out to the synagogues. What was good for Vermont would be good enough for Louisiana.

One synagogue was receptive, but then had to backtrack after realizing they had a full agenda. Another synagogue said they would be happy to have me, but that they were Messianic Jews. That was a line I was not willing to cross.

I then found one rabbi whose name I desperately wish I could remember. If he ever reads this book, I owe him a major apology for not mentioning him or his synagogue. It was not an Orthodox synagogue, which is all I recall. We had a philosophical discussion that was as fascinating as it was amusing.

He started by asking me about just visiting all fifty states. He wanted to know what I thought to that age-old travel question. Do airports count? If somebody has a stopover in an airport but never leaves the airport, does that count as having visited the state?

If one really wants to split hairs finer than they ever need to be split, the issue could be whether there is a change of planes during the stopover. Are the passengers staying on the airplane? If they exit the plane and walk to a different gate to catch their connecting flight, they have touched down on the ground of that state. Thankfully the rabbi and I never got that picayune.

Gate changes did not matter because I told the rabbi that in my world, airports do not count. One has to go somewhere, even if it means walking outside the airport and heading to the nearest town across the street. The rabbi said that in his world, airports do count. That could not change my calculus.

"Rabbi, I respect your opinion. However, this is not a Torah issue but a subjective standard about a non-religious issue. I cannot just alter my belief to fit a lower standard than I have always believed. I wish I believed that airports count, but I have always said they do not. I have to stick with that."

I wanted to know why this even mattered, and he quickly and quite brilliantly connected the dots.

"Eric, we have zero room in the Friday night program for even five minutes of speeches. I'd be glad to let you speak Saturday at lunch but you said you were unavailable. I have one idea. There is a part of the Friday night service where we give thanks. Every single congregant quickly stands up and says their name and what they are thankful for. There are no filibusters. You could do that and then after the service make friends with the people who stick around. What do you think?"

I made what I believed to be the right call. "Rabbi, that is beyond gracious of you. Unfortunately, that would be an airport. I could never convince myself that it would count. If I cannot find anything else I would be honored to join your congregation for Friday night Shabbos, but it would not count for my speaking. I need to go find something quickly."

I reached out to Rabbi Mendel Rivkin of Chabad of New Orleans. He was very friendly but had no room in his program that Friday night. He referred me to Rabbi Yossi Nemes of Chabad of Metairie, a New Orleans suburb. This was my last hope unless I wanted to spend Friday night yelling at strangers on Bourbon Street in exchange for beads. For purposes of checking off states, that would not count.

I met Rabbi Nemes at his Chabad House and told him I had the strangest dilemma he had probably ever heard. He suggested that I come to services. While he did not have room for speeches during the Friday night service, I was welcome to join him, his family and other guests at his home after the service for a Shabbos meal. When I told him about the conversation with the other rabbi concerning airports, he totally understood. Many people at his table gave short speeches about Judaism. He gave me a few minutes to give an actual speech.

I shared the same couple of Chabad stories I told in Vermont. I then sat back with a look of relief. An amused Rabbi Nemes suggested I tell everyone why it was so important for me to tell those stories. I quickly retold my story of my difficulty in being able to give the speech, the exact story I just told here. In all I spoke for more than five and less than ten minutes.

In December of 2014 I returned to New Orleans on business. I returned to Chabad of New Orleans and put on tefillin with Rabbi Rivkin. I thanked him for his help. I then returned to Chabad of Metairie and profusely thanked Rabbi Nemes. He invited me over for dinner again, and this time I was happy to not speak and just listen.

The highlight of the night was when he got one line of a Jewish song stuck in his head. It quickly became stuck in my head. "Zochreini na, Zochreini na, ve'chazkeini na..."[68] The song by Dov Shurin is about Samson asking Hashem to help him defeat the Philistines. That is the only line I know. Now it is stuck in your head as well. To get rid of it, replace it with, "Young folks, old folks, everybody come..."

After speaking in all fifty states, I went back to the stunning Jewish brunette who encouraged me to start my blog. I told her I would give up all of the money, praise, and D-List celebrity fame if she and I could just be a happy couple. She told me I was great at faking sincerity, which is why she believed in me to begin with. "I am your biggest fan. Go make your money." I lost the girl, made the money, and have never been happier (sorry mom and dad).

As 2015 approached, there was still one thing missing. Despite achieving a national presence, I had done almost no speaking to Jewish audiences. Well over ninety-nine percent of my audiences were Christian. I figured there was far less money to be made speaking in synagogues than at political events, but I wanted to spend time with my own Jewish people. My career had been established. It was time to find the love of my life and become a husband and father.

Many Christian women over the years have heard me speak and shown me pictures of their daughters and granddaughters. I politely thanked them but explained that I was looking for a Jewish woman. Speaking in the synagogues would help me from a career standpoint and a personal standpoint. While I could theoretically spend more time in shul without speaking, my career puts food on my table.

Some synagogues will not touch politics for a variety of reasons. I respect that. Other synagogues will allow politics only if both sides are represented.

I have done presidential debates in synagogues where I represented one candidate and my friend represented the other one. The congregants enjoyed the discussion. It was very healthy for synagogue attendees to see that two friends could completely disagree on issues while still loving each other and breaking bread afterward.

While I enjoy political discussions, my core is a guy who likes to make people laugh. Humor is humor. I can do political humor without crossing the line into outright advocacy. My mostly partisan humor can become non-partisan with slight tweaks.

An even bigger leap is just doing humor that has nothing to do with politics. I prefer telling stories, not jokes. My Jewish upbringing provided me with plenty of stories. You have spent time absorbing some of them, hopefully with joy.

I will still give political speeches, but it is time to regularly enter the synagogues across America. One way to spread this message is through social media. This brings me to one of my favorite Chabad rabbis, Mendy Mangel of Cherry Hill, New Jersey.

When I met Mendy, putting on tefillin with him was just a joy. Now whenever I am in a city traveling, I seek out a Chabad rabbi to help me put on tefillin. I could do it myself, but I like the feel of entering the Chabad House and performing the ritual in the sanctuary. Mendy encouraged me to actively pursue speaking opportunities in the synagogues. He told me I would be fine crossing over from politics to other forms of humor. I was nervous when I started my speaking career, but that turned out fine. If I could succeed before receiving help from Chabad rabbis, the sky is the limit with their support.

Mendy asked my permission to take a picture of me wearing tefillin and then post it to Facebook. I figured if he ever became famous, I could brag to people that I put on tefillin with him. I told him I would be honored. When posting the picture to my own Facebook page, I added my favorite Jewish comment. "It is easy to be this handsome when you belong to a religion this beautiful."

It is easy to find Judaism this beautiful when there are so many great rabbis out there spreading this beauty. The rabbis would most likely say that it is easy to spread this beauty because it comes from Hashem. As a speaker, I would certainly speak to that. The key to successful speaking is to speak from the heart. I love Judaism and look forward to sharing my Jewish stories with the world. Earning money doing it and meeting a nice Jewish girl would certainly be additional bonuses.

Chapter 12: Internal Jewish Lunacy: Too Jewish vs. not Jewish enough

There are approximately twelve Jews in America. Three live in New York and three more are in Los Angeles. Texas and Florida have two apiece. One of them ended up in North Dakota while the other one is roaming around somewhere. While the actual number is slightly higher than twelve, it is still frightening how few Jews exist. In a world of seven billion people, Christianity, Islam, Hinduism and Buddhism all claim at least one billion adherents. There are fourteen million Jews, or one-fifth of one percent of the world's population.[69]

The fifty-two percent intermarriage rate among Jews is decimating the Jewish community. It is easy to make excuses when 99.8% of people are not Jewish to begin with. This excuse is hollow. There are plenty of Jews in New York and Los Angeles, but nothing has stopped the hemorrhaging of our people out of the religion.

For many Jews determined to marry other Jews, being Jewish is not enough. Some Jews are too Jewish. Others are not Jewish enough. This intra-religious cannibalism is sometimes based on deep convictions that matter. Other times it is based on nonsense. The key is to know the difference.

Throughout my dating life, women have referred to me as being too Jewish and not Jewish enough. As a sweet Catholic girl asked me in 1997, "What the heck is wrong with you guys? Beggars can't be choosers."

The issue is more complex than that, but far simpler than the complainers think. Life is simple. People make it complicated. Jewish people are no exception.

Goldiberglocks and the three Jews: Baby Bear was just right Jewish

Back in the 1990s a buddy of mine and I took a pair of twins out on a double date. While one twin was very interested in my friend, the other girl quietly told her parents her concern about me. She was less quiet than she thought. "Mom, he has long hair."

Normally it is the parents raising that as a red flag. This was the reverse. The mom liked me and said, "Honey, your father had long hair when I met him." When the girl brought up my hair again, her mother cut her off and said, "Let it go. He's a stockbroker." At first I thought the mom was being supportive. I then realized she saw a young, rich, successful guy.

The daughter knew nothing about me and should not have jumped to a negative conclusion. The mother knew just as little about me and should not have jumped to a positive conclusion. Stockbrokers can have long hair. I was a stockbroker in Beverly Hills. I was not rich. I have made money, spent money and maintained the same friends my whole life. They liked me when I was struggling and when I was prospering. My romantic life was out of my control and far more complicated than it ever needed to be.

Some guys are scared of commitment, but I never was. I always wanted to be a husband and father but my workaholic nature put my career first. The date with that twin struck the wrong kind of chord. After the double date ended, my buddy J.J. drove the girls home and spoke to me when we were alone in his car.

"Eric, the long hair worried her in the beginning but you won her over. She liked you. However, she probably will not go out with you again because of something that happened over dinner. It wasn't your fault but you should know the truth." I listened, since I knew J.J. had my back.

"When the waiter came to take our order, you asked if he could serve you the beef taco plate without cheese. You did not want to mix milk and meat. That freaked her out. She was worried you were religious."

Logic is a lost skill. More people should learn it. "J.J., that is insane. Why would she think that? We were in a non-kosher restaurant. The meat was not kosher. Trying not to mix milk and meat so I can obey some semblance of kosher hardly makes me religious. I was barely keeping kosher-style. A religious guy would not even be in that restaurant."

J.J. tried to help. "Look, I tried to explain that to her but she was still worried."

Something else went off inside me. I was trying to prove I was not religious. Why would I do this? If I had been religious, what would be the problem with that? Why would that be wrong? Why should I be ashamed for trying to do something positive?

I was proud to be Jewish and could not understand why any self-respecting Jewish woman would object to that. Then I remembered that many Jews are not self-respecting.

Unfortunately, my moral stand quickly disappeared. Expediency replaced integrity when the next girl came along. Lowy was a goddess of grace, class and beauty. All the beauty in the world will not make a woman classy. Lowy was exquisite, elegant to the core. Naturally I attempted to get to know her. The telephone conversation went fine until I inserted my very unkosher feet into my mouth.

"By the way, don't worry about the Judaism thing. I am not religious. I eat what I want, and can take you anywhere you want. I have no restrictions, so whatever puts a smile on your face works for me."

She ended the conversation politely and told me we would talk again, but I knew something was wrong. A couple of hours later a mutual friend called me. "Eric, what did you do?"

I did not see the problem. "I calmed her down by assuring her I was not religious. I did not want her to start panicking about all that kosher and Shabbos stuff." That was not a good move.

"Eric, she is Orthodox. Now she will never go out with you. Why would you say such a thing?"

How was I supposed to know she was Orthodox? In my uneducated world where television hyper-sexualized everything, religious people were supposed to look and act as modest as the characters from *Little House on the Prairie*.[70] Orthodox girls could not look hot, and they certainly could not look sexy. Could they?

Young men could be imbeciles, and I was no exception. Just because Orthodox people keep their desires and passions private does not mean they lack them. Dignified does not equal dispassionate. Orthodox women want to be physically desired. They just want that lust to come from their husbands in the context of a loving marriage. That knowledge sure could have been useful to me a couple of decades ago.

I made one last attempt to undo the damage with Lowy. I told her about attending Camp Gan Yisroel, meeting the Lubavitcher Rebbe, and being the head cantor at my Orthodox shul in my youth. "My grandfather was an Orthodox rabbi. My other grandfather was even more religious. I am from an Orthodox background."

Lowy was sweet but asked a couple of obvious questions. "Eric, why didn't you tell me this upfront? Why hide that stuff if you are proud of it?"

For once I did the smart thing and remembered that less is more. "I messed up Lowy. Lovely women sometimes take a guy's brain and turn it into mush. I can be intelligent when I choose to be."

She asked the one question I feared the most. She heard what I said, but pounced on what I did not say. "Eric, I know you are a smart guy. I believe you when you say you are from an Orthodox background. I also believe what you said the first time we spoke. You had all this religious education. What happened to you? Where did it go?"

All I could tell her was that it was a long story. I wrestle with the issue seriously. She appreciated my honesty but noted that this was not the same as answering her question. She told me again that she thought I was a great guy that she would not be going out with. I shielded her from the truth, but not because of sexism. She was tough enough to handle it. I just knew the answer was a soulless one. It was better that she thought well of me and turned me down than thought ill of me and turned me down.

Issues such as romance and religion should be based on deep convictions and emotions. My level of religiosity became a cold, ruthless calculation. I crunched the numbers. Sixty to seventy percent of Jewish women were secular. Ten percent of them were religious.[71] My chances of meeting a secular Jewish woman I clicked with was six or seven times greater than experiencing this with an Orthodox woman. Presto, I was secular.

This was probably the worst decision I ever made in terms of Judaism. 6,000 years of tradition took a back seat to statistical analysis with flawed data. Rather than mathematical numbers, perhaps I should have studied the Book of Numbers. Maybe I should have learned the difference between quality and quantity.

While there are plenty of emotionally healthy non-Orthodox women who are ready for marriage, there are also many non-Orthodox women with other priorities. Their careers often come first. Some women just want to have causal relationships. Modern feminism has played a major role in blurring the lines between the sexes. Women are taught that acting as carnal and ambitious as men will bring them equality. Sometimes it does, but in many cases that equality is just equal misery.

Women and men are different. Women have biological urges. Many women yearn to be wives, mothers and homemakers. They do not find this degrading or a form of enslavement. In the Orthodox world, particularly among the Chasidim, being a domestic wife is empowering. They control the home and everything that comes into it. Chasidic women are born and bred to be good wives. The men are trained how to be good husbands. It is their major career decision. The job that brings them income is a secondary means to an end. The married lifestyle matters far more. While secular women are larger in numbers, religious women are far more prepared to get married and raise children.

Knowing what to do is hard enough. Converting noble sentiments into proper deeds is far more difficult. A 2005 conversation with a Muslim offered a valuable perspective. My former boss saw me working one Saturday. My goal was to accrue enough overtime hours to earn extra vacation days. His question was a simple one.

"Eric, you're Jewish. Tell me this. Greg in Chicago is Jewish. He never works on Saturday. How come you do?"

There were plenty of long-winded answers I could have given. All of them would have been awful. I could have explained that Greg was religious and I was not. I hated that answer because listening to Jews say they are not religious sickens me. When asked if they are Jewish, far too many Jews defensively respond, "Yes, but I'm not religious." I instantly think, "I didn't ask you that." Why do so many Jews say this? Christians do not respond this way. Why are so many Jews so scared to be associated with Judaism? Many Jews openly brag about eating bagels, watching Seinfeld[72], and enjoying Christmas. This comes across as a desperate attempt to assimilate for fear of being rejected by Christians. Christians are proud of who they are. They respect Jews who show that same pride in being Jewish. With my Muslim boss, the simplest answer was the right answer. "I'm not supposed to."

That was truthful. I was more interested in making money than keeping Shabbos. If I knew this was wrong, why not just stop doing it? This is where the struggle came to a head. Pick a cliché. The rubber met the road. A conversation with a Muslim friend named Faisal crystallized everything. He was very intelligent and knew some basic facts about Judaism. He wanted to know why being labeled a Reform Jew bothered me so much if I did not obey many Jewish laws.

"Faisal, I reject the Reform label for myself. I respect that other people are fine with it, but I am not. Reform Judaism, and I am making some generalizations here, often says the traditions are obsolete. Kosher laws are a product of a bygone era. This is the twenty-first century. The traditions no longer apply. Faisal, I don't believe this. The traditions are not wrong. I am wrong. Do I keep kosher and Shabbos? No. Should I? Yes. How come I don't? I don't know. What I do know is that I am not going to blame the traditions for my shortcomings."

This Jew and his religious Muslim friend then bonded over watching Al Bundy in *Married with Children*.

I put it more succinctly in a similar conversation with my Chasidic friend Nate. "Nate, I don't obey halachah because I'm a screw-up. That's it." He disagreed. He said that we are all struggling to improve. I hope he was more right than me.

I wish there was a term called rebel Orthodox or non-practicing Orthodox. This struggle of watching people be labeled too Jewish or not Jewish enough allowed me to help dear friends of mine in ways I refused to help myself.

In college, my modern Orthodox friend had a very secular girlfriend. He kept breaking up with her because she was not religious enough. Then he would take her back. I warned him that she would eventually give up on him. One day I saw him crying in the lounge. "Eric, she is not coming back this time. She is gone forever."

I should have been supportive, but instead I unloaded. "I told you if you ever lost that girl that you would never forgive yourself. You need to fix this. You have to talk to her face to face. If you have to break into her apartment and risk getting arrested, do what you have to do. When you get in front of her, let her know who is boss."

He curiously asked me how to do that.

"You're going to get on your knees and cry like a four-year-old girl. You are going to cry your eyes out and not stop. You are going to clutch onto her leg until she demands you get up. Then you are going to get her some flowers. Forget this dozen roses nonsense. Her entire apartment should look like the Tournament of Roses Parade. She should not be able to move without bumping into flowers. Then you are going to go to the jewelry store and mortgage your entire future by buying her whatever diamond she wants."

They are now happily married with kids. When anyone asks how he won her back, he is not shy about telling the truth. "I cried like a baby. I would do it again." He may have done the crying, but he stayed modern Orthodox. She became more religious and moved in his direction when she was ready.

Another situation thankfully did not require tears. The scenario was the same. He was modern orthodox and she was secular. He was worried that he was on the verge of losing her. He told me that all he wanted was to make her happy. Whatever she wanted was fine with him. She was still unsure. She sat with me in my car and told me what bothered her.

"Eric, I don't want religion rammed down my throat. I do not want religious Judaism forced on me."

Her point would be valid with some guys, but not with the one she was seeing. "Has he ever tried to force his religiosity on you even once?" She conceded that he had not.

"Hasn't he told you many times that whatever makes you happy makes him happy?"

She admitted that he did say this.

"Do you think he's lying?" She knew he was a good, decent and honest man.

"Do you love him or are you looking for a way out?" She did love him.

"Let's review. We live in a world where many people spend their entire lives looking for somebody to unconditionally love and accept them. You have a man who thinks the sun rises and sets based on your happiness. He wants to spend the rest of his life making you happy whatever it takes. He has never asked you to change and loves you just the way you are. Do you think you may be inventing a problem that does not exist and will not exist?"

She heeded my words. "Do you think the streets are crawling with good guys like this? Do you think most men are this patient and understanding?"

She knew that was not the case. "If he crosses the line, then deal with that. If he keeps his word, you owe a good man the benefit of the doubt. You won the lottery. Go cash in your winning ticket."

They got engaged. Then one thing changed. The next time I saw them, I went to hug her as I had many times before. She stopped me and said, "Eric, I can't hug you. I'm getting married." She was now Shomer Negiah! I gave him a bear hug and her an air hug from across the room. Without any prodding from him, she moved toward him and even past him on the religious spectrum. He became slightly more religious so that they would both be Chasidic. They now have six children.

Jews need to figure out what they want. As children their parents can guide them. As adults we have to make our own decisions and accept the ramifications. I have said in recent years that I do not need to make a decision on my level of religiosity. My wife will have ninety-five to ninety-nine percent of the say in what type of home we have. If she wants to eat bacon-cheeseburgers and keep a secular house, fine with me. If she wants a Chasidic home, fine by me. I just want my wife to be happy. While this may come across as flexible, it sadly may not work.

At some point a man may have to just man up and stand for something. He has to decide who he is, and only after that is he right for the right woman. Most Orthodox women would not consider me until I was Orthodox. I would become observant for myself, not for her. A secular woman would not want a man to give up his religiosity for her. I could try and find somebody with the same internal dilemma that I have, but that could be too much to ask.

I keep saying, could, may, and possibly, because when all is said and done, much is said and nothing has been done. I know what I should do but have no idea when or even if I will do it. I know right from wrong. Knowing and analyzing are thoughts and words. The deeds have not been done. I remain a proud Jew who does not obey Jewish laws.

Chapter 13: Vocational Lunacy: More stockbrokers, fewer teachers and social workers

Jews are known as, "The People of the Book."[73] Jews are considered intelligent, studious, and dedicated to learning. Judaism has become synonymous with education. Jews also have a strong commitment to helping others who are struggling. Our history of oppression makes us sensitive toward the downtrodden. Jews are among the first people to help alleviate human suffering.

While these twin commitments to education and healing the world are positive on the surface, deep down they sometimes do more harm than good. It is one thing to help people. It is another to make that a career choice at the expense of personal financial security. God helps those who help themselves, and the Jewish community has been committing financial self-immolation that is every bit as destructive as our cultural self-immolation.

To preserve Judaism and help the world, Jews must go into financially lucrative careers. Jews must embrace corporate America. The next time they get the urge to become schoolteachers and social workers and save the world, they need to just let Christians handle that.

Jewish Tikkun Olam: Let the Christians handle it

As the son of two retired schoolteachers, I see the Jewish people on the way to slow disintegration one public schoolteacher or social worker at a time. When I speak to young Jewish individuals, I beg them not to become schoolteachers (unless they can luck into working at wealthy private schools), social workers or entertainment industry personnel. The survival of the Jewish people depends on avoiding these professions. There are three reasons for this.

The first reason is economic. The pay is dreadful. Jewish people have political power in America because of economic power gained through business success. We were bankers, and more importantly, merchants. Jews excelled in import-export and other trade-related professions from agriculture to textiles to precious metals. Jews nowadays, especially Jewish women, gravitate toward professions that may be noble but are disastrously low on the socioeconomic scale. No girl grows up dreaming of a life of economic insecurity, longer hours, frustrating bureaucracy, and supervisors enforcing rigid routines where creativity equals rebellion. The era of the creative teacher is long gone. Teachers spend hours working on lesson plans that must conform to a central plan approved by their high commanders.

Schoolteachers often complain that star athletes can make millions while educators struggle. Only several hundred people are qualified to play professional sports. Every year the players get stronger and tougher. The standards get higher. In education, standards keep getting lower. This allows more people to become teachers, lowering the market value of the entire profession. Supply and demand works. If enough people would refuse to become teachers, shortages would trigger a rise in pay levels.

College professors can earn six-figure salaries, but professors are not teachers. Publish or perish separates a cushy tenured life from a mediocre one. Professors spend several hours a week teaching and the rest of their time engaging in self-aggrandizing pursuits designed to enhance their own portfolios. People have every right to devote their lives to their own selfish causes. The sin is the denial. For some reason college professors refuse to admit that they do this, offering pabulum about noble pursuits and the greater good. The lecture circuit is lucrative. Research can be, and is often subsidized. Actual teaching is neither.

Then again, schoolteachers are financial geniuses compared to social workers. Some people find it fulfilling to spend twelve to fourteen hours every day observing families on the verge of destruction. While social workers earn very little pay, at least they get endless heartache as a tradeoff. One cannot pay bills or feed a family on emotional agony.

The entertainment industry is the worst. Actors and producers can make millions. So can lottery winners. The many who get destroyed in pursuit of a dream few ever attain end up getting washed away by the glorification of the few who succeed. Unlike professional sports, Hollywood is not a meritocracy.

Jewish moms still pray that their daughters marry doctors and lawyers. Prayers would be unnecessary if their daughters would become doctors and lawyers themselves. They should become corporate lawyers and not legal aid lawyers. Hired guns willing to defend tobacco companies, gun manufacturers, fast food companies and alcohol distillers earn high salaries, corner offices, and healthy bonuses.

While many Jewish women choose to become homemakers, other women want careers. Career women need to become investment bankers, stockbrokers, international trade merchants, corporate lawyers, and accountants. They need to become salespeople. Whether they sell insurance, automobiles or beauty products is irrelevant.

Career women need to learn skills that allow them to charge whatever they want. How many Jewish women become plumbers, electricians, auto mechanics or carpenters? Jewish moms may find these blue-collar jobs beneath their daughters, but we give hundreds of thousands of dollars to these people because we cannot change our oil, fix a sink, or install any system. The plumber not good enough to be the son-in-law earns more than the schoolteacher because the plumber's income is unlimited.

The second reason for the education-disintegration link is also economic. However, it is the cause and not the effect. It is the means, not the end. The concept is risk. Risk-takers founded America. The Pilgrims had to succeed. Failure meant death. Through wars, famines, pestilences and bad harvests, they learned skills. They lacked advanced business degrees from Harvard yet were educated in life survival. The Founding Fathers risked everything when they declared independence from the French (Just checking to see if you were paying attention. Heaven only knows what today's schoolchildren are learning or failing to learn).

America is about entrepreneurship where risk-takers can be rewarded, often quite handsomely. Jews, again primarily the women, are frequently risk-averse in their professional choices. Teaching is risk aversion personified. Teachers receive a safe paycheck, have a safe work schedule, and are condemned to a safe life. In the business world this safety is referred to as mediocrity. Truly blessed teachers can become assistant principals, then principals, and even superintendents. This is rare. Those decisions are political. Cronyism exists. Education is not a meritocracy because so many people are qualified to be teachers. When athletes succeed they get bonuses and rich contracts. Good teachers are rewarded with the worst students because they can handle them. The worst teachers get the best students because that is all they can handle. This hurts teachers and students.

The Internet age can be a financial lifeline. It has allowed entrepreneurship to flourish. Home-based businesses are booming. Startup costs are low and barriers to entry are even lower. From eBay to Craigslist to anythingyoucanimagine.com (Go ahead and use it), the options and income potential are limitless. The major requirement is the ability to take far less risk than the Pilgrims needed to take.

Social workers are not risk-takers unless one counts showing up at the home of their cases, also known as potential death threats. There is risk, but financially where is the reward? There is all downside and no economic upside. The entertainment industry has an element of risk, but it is not a calculated risk. Skill is outweighed by luck. This risk is akin to jumping off of a bridge in the hopes of flying.

When Jews become teachers and social workers, they inadvertently (and sometimes intentionally) force their own limited worldview on their innocent victims. My teachers did not influence me to try and succeed on Wall Street. I did that on my own. My teachers taught that safety, security and being part of a successful collective would bring happiness. Successful individualism is still discouraged. Bright students are forced to slow down so that slower students do not have their feelings hurt. How can children become entrepreneurial if teachers exist outside of that foreign world?

The third reason why Jewish people need to stop going into the education and social work fields is politics. These professions are overwhelmingly political. Jews often complain about how little society supposedly contributes to education. Why should we? If somebody brought me an investment guaranteed to cost more money while giving inferior results, I would quickly hide my wallet. Giving more money to public education is not the answer. The solution is for people to stop going into these professions to begin with. When America as a whole becomes desperate, only then can the system be improved.

American colleges and universities are the envy of the world because of competition and the free market. Colleges fight for top professors. They offer financial incentives to do what would otherwise be a thankless job. This works.

Children need to learn a cold-blooded reality that most schoolteachers will not share with them. Life is ruthless and cutthroat. Life swallows up children expecting someone to save them. Ask European Jews who went through the 1930s about the benefits of trusting your neighbor to help you enjoy life. The tough Jews relied on themselves. Those who escaped to America knew that survival costs money. They began the task of making lots of money one risk and one dollar at a time.

Saying there is more to life than making money is not the same as declaring money unimportant. People who truly believe money is unimportant should be commended. They go to Africa and other poor areas to help blind kids see. They run soup kitchens and homeless shelters. Despite barely subsisting themselves, they feel good and probably merit entry into heaven well before most people, myself included.

However, carpenters know how to build soup kitchens. Investment bankers can raise the money to create larger soup kitchens and bigger and better shelters. Electricians can set up the lights. Rich people give more money to charity than poor people because they have it.

Many Jews, particularly women, light up when helping people. Tikkun Olam guides them. Happiness trumps money. They would be taken more seriously if their mothers were not demanding they marry high achievers. Loving mothers do not want their children eating snow (grass or dirt if you live in Los Angeles) for dinner.

Jewish America must wake up. The best way to help people and live a quality life is by getting wealthy. Wealth can create more wealth. Many of the one billion Christians in this world believe that Jesus commands them to help the poor through labors of love. Let Christians spend their lives on the downtrodden. Jews do not have the manpower. There are too few of us. We need to help ourselves or we will cease to exist as a people.

Until Jews are on the streets panhandling en masse, this will not be taken seriously. We Jews are on the edge. Mortgages are getting expensive. College tuition and healthcare costs are skyrocketing. Vacations are a thing of the past for many. Living paycheck to paycheck is becoming the norm. The 2008 financial crisis devastated many formerly wealthy families. Once the economic power goes, political power is gone. This is true for individuals, religions, and nations. Jews must stop becoming public schoolteachers, social workers or entertainment industry dreamers and get high-paying jobs. Our future survival depends on it.

Ben Affleck in *Boiler Room* said it best. "You think money doesn't make me happy? Look at the (flipping) smile on my face."[74]

Hashem helps those who help themselves. Young Jews need to quit focusing on downtrodden people who far too often do not appreciate the efforts rendered. By entering the business world, Jews can build empires and live happily ever after as Jewish kings and queens used to live. Then they can give back and heal many more people for far longer.

Chapter 14: Political Lunacy: The Torah is non-partisan

America is more politically divided than ever. So are Israel and many other democracies. For political harmony, North Korea and Saudi Arabia are lovely during the spring. Men who sharply disagreed with each other founded America. Jews have never been about consensus. "Two Jews, three opinions" is as old as thought itself.

The problem comes when people cannot turn off their political passions. They confuse opponents with enemies and allow their activist causes to result in their ignoring everything around them. This destroys families.

I am as politically passionate as anybody. If I can put my politics aside in writing an entire book, you the reader can put yours aside for a precious few pages.

There is nothing wrong with being political or religious. There is everything wrong with trying to conflate these two distinct sets of beliefs. It is deeply offensive to use the Torah to justify a political ideology. Hashem wrote the Torah. Hashem does not care who wins an American presidential election.

Jesus was not a Republican and Moses was not a Democrat

Many non-Orthodox Jews are terrified of evangelical Christians. That fear frequently crosses the line into hostility emanating from staunch disagreements on political social issues like abortion and gay rights. Non-Orthodox Jews and evangelical Christians have sharp disagreements, especially among their respective women.

The secular Jewish complaint usually centers on criticism of America's Christian churches. Churches have supposedly devolved from institutes of religious holiness to shadow vehicles for the Republican Party and politically conservative causes.

There have been horrendous acts. My longest friend since we were six years old is a proud Christian. He also announced to the world in 2014 that he is a proud gay man. He is not a political activist. This was not good enough for his local church that ex-communicated him. This terrible act by one church must not invalidate all churches. It must certainly not be used as a cudgel to demonize all Christians. My friend is a gay Christian. Many secular Jews who would never dare criticize his sexuality would attack his religion without blinking an eye.

The refrain from these Jews is that Jesus was not a Republican.[75] The Torah does take issue with homosexuality, but it also preaches compassion for the poor, the weak and the sick among us. Pope Francis has earned high praise from liberals for focusing more on charity than social issues. Unfortunately these same secular Jews often have zero problem turning synagogues into Democrat Party headquarters. Their justification is the Torah teaching social justice, environmental justice, and equality for all in the eyes of God.

The Torah actually says none of this. The Torah wants us to be charitable but does not promote wealth redistribution. Being good stewards of the earth does not mandate increased regulations on carbon emissions, cap and trade legislation, or even caring about climate change. Nothing in the Torah demanding compassion for the weak, sick and poor requires vilifying the rich.

Now flip the coin. Look at some of the most serious issues of the day. Look at the liberal and conservative positions. Then look at the Torah and see which side it appears to favor.

Capital punishment used to divide along clear ideological lines. Then some conservatives began backing away from supporting the death penalty due to religious beliefs. Some liberals began supporting the death penalty for extreme cases such as terrorism. While less rigidly ideological than before, the death penalty is still generally supported by conservatives and a source of consternation for liberals.

The Torah is very clear. Capital punishment in many situations is justified.[76] No honest interpretation would allow arguing otherwise.

Welfare is another divisive issue. While there was a brief consensus in the 1990s, the political parties have reverted back to their traditional positions in recent years. Liberals see welfare as a way of helping those who need it most. Conservatives see the current welfare system as a destructive force that traps poor people in an endless cycle of dependency.

The teachings of Pirkei Avos explicitly state that justice is supposed to be blind, cold and even-handed. Stealing or confiscating property from a rich person to give to a poor person is prohibited.[77] The Torah is a guideline for how Hashem wants individuals to treat each other. It does not in any way ever give any government the right to substitute its judgment for that of private individuals.

Tzedakah is the noblest Jewish deed, greater than all other mitzvahs combined. One of the biggest misconceptions among Jews is that tzedakah means charity. Tzedakah is *justice*, with another synonym being *righteousness*.[78]

Political liberals cite the word justice when trying to convert their beliefs to policies. There is social justice, economic justice, environmental justice, and many other justices. The word justice is then translated to mean *equality*. This leads to liberal activism on behalf of marriage equality, gender equality and racial equality and against income inequality.

Tzedakah is derived from tzedek, which translates into justice, righteousness, and one other word: fairness. For liberals, fairness is an aspirational goal and a justification for policy prescriptions. Liberals deeply believe in using government to spread fairness and improve lives.

Moses Maimonides offers a starkly different view. The RaMBaM teaches that there are eight different levels of tzedakah. Anonymous gifts between givers and receivers are only the second highest level. The greatest level of tzedakah is helping somebody going into business so they can become self-sufficient.[79] Teaching people how to fish rather than just giving them a fish is the heart of the modern politically conservative message.

Rich people can, should and do give to charity for reasons of their choosing. Government coercion and confiscation of wealth is not charity. True charity is voluntary. Tzedakah is not voluntary. It is a religious obligation all Jews must perform whether rich or poor.

No Jewish text plays favorites based on financial status. Only governments do. There is no link between religious Jewish texts and secular governing bodies. The Torah does not justify action taken by any executive, legislature, judiciary, administrative agency or media institution. The Torah frequently offers advice that directly counters those desiring an activist government.

Does this discredit liberalism and vindicate conservatism?

No. What is does is discredit the notion that liberalism or conservatism emanate from the Torah. This should be self-evident, but political activists are often blind to the obvious. The solution is not to vilify liberalism or conservatism but to honestly admit where they both come from. Liberalism and conservatism are political ideologies formed during the political socialization process, which comes from human beings. These people are parents, teachers or other mere mortals. The Torah comes from Hashem. Its words are spiritual and legal, not political.

People have every right to their politics. It is deeply offensive and a complete misunderstanding of Torah to use the Torah or any other Jewish texts to justify any political point of view. To paraphrase Yogi Berra, people believe politically what they believe politically because they believe it, not because Hashem told them to believe it.

Jesus was never a conservative Republican. Moses was never a liberal Democrat. Anyone claiming otherwise is substituting their own judgment for the God in who they claim their subservience and obedience.

Chapter 15: Pacifist Lunacy: Hanukkah, the Six-Day War and the IDF

The Jewish faith is steeped in peace. Jews pray for peace in every service thrice daily. Sadly for Jews, there are other cultures containing vast numbers of people desiring everything but peace. Some people just want to kill the Jews. It was never about Israel or Zionists. The goal is to eliminate the Jew. Why the Jew? Why not? At this point it is tradition. There is nothing Jews can do to change this. Their history of being persecuted has given Jews a heightened sense of empathy. Empathy can be a positive quality, but not when it becomes misplaced. Evil exists. Large swaths of people are not redeemable. Jews are constantly being asked to make the hard choices necessary for peace. Those seeking to kill the Jews are given every benefit of the doubt. Agreements are broken as Jews are asked to sign new agreements that also end up broken.

Peace as a goal is laudable. Peace at any price is naïveté. Peace is when indiscriminate killing stops. Pacifism leads to brutal indiscriminate killings on a massive scale. It is sad that it takes a fictional character in a comic book movie to be the voice of reason, but Michael Caine's Alfred the Butler offers sound advice in 2008's *Batman: The Dark Knight*.

"Some men aren't looking for anything logical, like money. They can't be bought, bullied, reasoned or negotiated with. Some men just want to watch the world burn."[80]

Judaism is about peace, but not pacifism. Jewish history is inseparable from triumphs that occurred in war. If Jews want to heal the world, they must first, foremost and at all costs stop those people trying to burn the world.

We fought wars, we won wars, let's light candles, let's eat

Somewhere along the line many American Jews forgot where they came from. They can look at old photo albums and name cities in Europe or the Middle East. Where we Jews came from traces back six millennia, not six decades.

Non-Jews often refer to Jews as God's chosen people, implying a certain unconventional approach to living. The Jewish story in many ways is ordinary, conventional and typical. We won blood triumphs. We were victorious in wars.

The story of Hanukkah is described to children as a miracle of Hashem. The Maccabees only had enough oil to last one day but the oil lasted eight days. While this story cannot be dismissed, Hanukkah celebrates a military victory. The Maccabees beat the daylights out of the Greeks.[81] Gorgias? Get out of here! Nicanor? Knock it off!

Equally if not more significant than what the Maccabees did is what they did not do. They did not ask the world community for permission to defend themselves. They acted unilaterally. They did not dialogue with the Greeks trying to exterminate the Jews. They skipped the soft power of pointless diplomacy and went straight to using hard military power. The Maccabean Jews did not seek out and try to maximize collateral damage, but they did not obsess over minimizing it. Collateral damage would be unfortunate, but not a deterrent.

The worst Jewish defeat was the Holocaust. Jews were not at war with their enemies, but that was precisely the problem. Our enemies were at war with us. We believed that if we just acted nicer and minded our manners, everything would turn out for the best. Jews got on boxcars because they believed the lies the Nazi government told them. Surely the world community would step in and save innocent people refusing to fight. Jews even voluntarily turned in their guns as a good faith gesture. The Warsaw Ghetto Jews who stocked up on weapons survived longer.[82] Many still died, but they eliminated some Nazis before their defeat.

Israel is often described as winning all five Arab-Israeli wars between 1948 and 2000 while engaging in self-defense. While this is technically true, the 1967 Six-Day War saw Israel officially fire first. The Arabs were about to attack, and Israelis decided not to wait and get killed. Israel engaged in a preemptive war.[83]

In 2000 Israel abandoned its policy of never rewarding Arab rejectionism. Israel voluntarily pulled out of Lebanon without preconditions. In 2005 Israel voluntarily left the Gaza Strip without preconditions. In both cases the Arabs saw these moves as weakness. Rather than lead to peace, Israel's enemies became more emboldened and[84] subjected Israel to more terrorism.

This is not about political labels such as Neoconservative, Paleoconservative, pacifist, or other foreign policy nomenclature. What matters in foreign policy is what matters in every issue, separating what works from what does not work.

Diplomacy advocates claim that experiences from so long ago cannot and should not be extrapolated into twenty-first century foreign policy. This is wrong. The tools of warfare have become modernized, but the rules of life and human nature have not changed.

Concepts such as preemptive war, regime change and unilateral action have been demonized. Neocon has been turned into a pejorative by some people looking to attack all military action, others looking to attack political conservatives, and still others looking for any excuse to demonize Jews.

This does not mean that diplomacy is always a waste of time. To say, "War is not the answer" is nonsense. Sometimes war absolutely is the answer. War is not always the answer. The key, to quote "The Gambler" Kenny Rogers is to "Know when to hold 'em and know when to fold 'em."[85]

Wars end under one of two conditions, checkmate or stalemate. In World War II and many other wars, one side determined that victory was hopeless. In the Korean War both sides concluded that winning was impossible. It took President Harry S. Truman dropping atomic bombs on Hiroshima and Nagasaki, but the Japanese surrendered and many more lives were saved.

If both sides have even the slightest hope of victory, war will continue. This explains the perpetual state of war between the Israelis and Palestinians. Jordan and Egypt got to the point where they were militarily and psychologically broken. The Israeli Jews won. The Arabs lost. Then came the peace. The Palestinians never got to this point because Israel never went the distance. In 1982 Israeli General Ariel Sharon wanted to go all the way to Damascus.[86] He was not Prime Minister so it was not his decision. Three decades later, the Assad family is still murdering innocent people inside and outside of Syria. Think of how many people would be alive today if the policy of regime change had removed Assad.

Diplomacy is valuable when each side has something the other side wants. In the tradition of the Bee Gees and John Travolta, sometimes just *Staying Alive*[87] is enough incentive. Many societies want to do more than just subsist. They want to acquire what capitalists for centuries have referred to as stuff. Americans love stuff. We buy stuff. We celebrated 1980s television shows like *Dallas* and *Dynasty*[88] for showing glamorous Americans and their opulent stuff. Robin Leach became a celebrity with his show *Lifestyles of the rich and famous*.[89]

The former Soviet Empire could be reasoned with once both nations realized that the other side did not want to blow up the world. The Russians wanted stuff, especially American stuff. They loved blue jeans and Beatles tapes.[90] No sentient American advocates bombing China. The Chinese worship at the altar of stuff. They are a bunch of J.R. Ewings from *Dallas* who want to own everything. A society that values stuff is a rational society that can be reasoned with. Societies and cultures that have no use for stuff are crazy.

The Iranian mullahs have zero interest in stuff. Neither do the Palestinians. Palestinians in Gaza were given beautiful stuff in 2005. Israel left functional and attractive greenhouses for the Palestinians to own. Those greenhouses could have been used to help develop the Palestinian economy. Modern Israel began as an agricultural society starting with orange groves. Israelis knew a thing or two about creating wonderment in the desert. Rather than use the greenhouses, the Palestinians blew them up.[91] Sane, rational actors would not do that.

The 2008 *Batman* movie was a direct metaphor for the Global War on Terror. Alfred the Butler's referencing people who just wanted to watch the world burn explained the exact people who could not be dealt with diplomatically.

The Maccabees were not humble. They fought to avoid being assimilated into Greek culture and then upon victory immediately adopted a Greek custom. Greeks named holidays after military victories. Jews did not. As soon as the Maccabean Jews defeated the Greeks, the holiday of Hanukkah to celebrate the Jewish victory was born.[92] Hanukkah is the Jewish version of America's July Fourth Independence Day. We fought. We won. Let's light candles and eat.

Jews were every bit as tough as other societies that took tough steps to win wars. Jews differed in how they conducted themselves after they won. The Maccabees did not enslave the Greeks, rape Greek women, ransack the towns, destroy the Greek historical artifacts, or deliberately burn children alive.

The Israeli military has never done those things. Palestinians have engaged in repeated blood libel accusations that are always debunked. Jews are not poisoning the water of Palestinian children or using white phosphorous to kill Palestinians. The accusations keep coming, and they keep being exposed as lies.[93]

Jews should pray for the noble goal of peace, hope for the best and prepare for the worst. If war is waged, it must be all-out war with such overwhelming force that it leads to a decisive, total and complete victory. Palestinians and the other Arab and Muslim societies funding them must conclude that victory is hopeless. That is what leads to lasting peace. That is not theoretical or aspirational. That is Israel with regards to Egypt and Jordan. That is empirical evidence.

One last note about war involves Israel's nickname. The Jewish state's enemies refer to Israel as Little Satan. The United States is the Great Satan.[94] America is not hated for supporting Israel. Israel is hated because it reminds her enemies of America. Their ultimate goal is total annihilation of the American way of life and the death of societies built on Judeo-Christian values. Therefore, America's approach to war must be based on all-out victory.

The greatest evil used to be the Nazis. Now is it radical Islamists. They are at war with us. We cannot and must not refuse to be at war with them. They want to light the world on fire and watch it burn. The only way to stop them is to actually stop them. In this vein, the American and Jewish stories are intertwined. The problems are identical. The solution must be identical, forceful and permanent.

The Maccabees were alpha males. They were not metrosexuals or momma's boys. They laid the blueprint for how to handle the enemy. Sylvester Stallone in *The Expendables* offered the most recent Maccabean iteration for handling the bad guys. "Track 'em. Find 'em. Kill 'em."[95]

Then we Americans and Jews can celebrate a holiday where we argue at the dinner table whether the force we used was too much, not enough, or just right. Most of us at the table will be glad to be alive while clearly understanding what kept us alive. We can even argue about the name for the new Hanukkah once the war is wrapped up with a nice victorious Hanukkah bow.

Chapter 16: Conspiracy Lunacy: The Zionist Crusader Alliance for World Domination

Opinion columnist Dr. Charles Krauthammer is a trained psychiatrist and proud Jew. Known for his astute analytical skills and lacerating wit, he has on more than one occasion poked fun at conspiracy theorists.

"We meet every month on the full moon at the Masonic Temple. We have the ritual: Karl (Rove) brings the incense, I bring the live lamb and the long knife, and we began with a pledge of allegiance to the Trilateral Commission."[96]

The Trilateral Commission along with the Bilderberg Group[97] and the Illuminati[98] are secret powerful forces that supposedly control everyone in the world and what we do. Nobody knows who they are or if they even exist. They may be so secret that even they do not know who they are or if they exist. The one thing linking these forces is that they are all Jews. Zionist merchants, bankers and moneylenders are responsible for everything from the Brinks heist to Restless Leg Syndrome.

To handle and defeat the crackpots, another secret society was formed. Headquartered in an undisclosed location in a nice part of Los Angeles, the Zionist Crusader Alliance for World Domination is conspiring against the conspirators. The ZCA is being revealed for the first time so its proper role in Jewish history can be analyzed and debated forever.

Bolder than the Bilderberg Group and more illuminated than the Illuminati, the ZCA may or may not be real in achieving its objectives that it may or may not have. While the ZCA did start out as a triumvirate, we only move onward, upward and forward, not laterally.

Our mission, if we actually have one, is completely crystal clear or imaginary. All the other anti-Semitic conspiracy organizations will wither into dust. The ZCA will live on forever. It will either be the greatest anti-conspiracy organization in history or a fictional entity that never existed. Driving the conspiracy theorists mad is not necessary. They are already stark raving mad. The ZCA's purpose, if there is one, is to use the bat-spit crazies as a foil to amuse the rest of us. At the very least, we have amused the three of us.

We would stay in the shadows but it is dark and scary over there

In 1990, my friend Eric and I were vice presidents of the Lethargy Club. President Jason literally slept his way to the top. He was a master nap-taker. The Lethargy Club leadership was also the complete membership. We watched football and fell asleep whenever we wanted. Unlike people who actively went to bars and got drunk, we just slept under the belief that it is always 5:00 a.m. somewhere. Our mascot was the Lethargizer Bunny, who just kept going and going until he stopped, fell down, and went to sleep. The Lethargy Club high-five was raising our arms and then being too tired to slap hands. We would just motion them as if to say, "Feh."

Jason left Los Angeles, but the Lethargy Club has been as dormant and inactive as ever the last twenty-five years. We are hard at the work of sleep.

Jason was somewhat political, but not as political as the two Erics. Our friend Brian is also political, and we needed to save the world during the times when naps were too hard to come by. Brian, Eric and I are the Zionist Crusader Alliance for World Domination.

Eric's experience with conspiracy lunatics came in the form of a roommate who believed that Jews were vampires. The guy poured garlic all over Eric's clothing.

Wackos are everywhere. In India a group of cultists were convinced that flat tires were the key to salvation.[99] They went around town slashing tires and bringing traffic to a standstill while letting the victims know that the lord loves them. Angry motorists may have screamed that the next time a flat tire cultist tried to send a motorist to heaven, the motorist would beat the hell out of them. Other unconfirmed rumors had copycat flat tire cultists coming to the Sherman Oaks area of the San Fernando Valley in Los Angeles.

I remember Palestinians crashing a pro-Israel rally at the Federal Building and calling me a "Donkey Zionist aggressor infidel!" I looked around for three other people until realizing I was supposedly all four of them. I grabbed the megaphone and said, "You people do not need a homeland. You need a thesaurus. I have heard better insults at the school parking lot at 3:00 p.m. after school and during recess."

Apparently my chanting, "Two, four, six, eight, you should never procreate" did not amuse them.

Brian plays his cards closer to the vest but also has no patience for conspiracy nuts.

Whoever these rich Jews controlling everything are, none of my friends have seven-figure bank accounts or sneakers made of gold. If my parents have been holding out on me all these years and really are wealthy, I will take back everything I ever said about public schoolteachers.

Most wealthy Jews in America are secular. Orthodox Jews are often on the verge of being broke. Feeding ten children and caring about an entire community of fellow Jews does not leave much money for buying platinum-encrusted Gefilte fish, which may or may not exist.

In addition to the BITs (Bilderberg Group, Illuminati and Trilateral Commission), Goldman Sachs is apparently part of the Zionist Conspiracy. Jon Corzine and Hank Paulson are offered as evidence, but neither of them have ever been Jewish. Perhaps this is part of the conspiracy. J.P. Morgan-Chase is also somehow connected to this massive global Jewish Wall Street conspiracy. Mr. Morgan was not Jewish. Neither is the current CEO Jamie Dimon.

Bill Gates, Paul Allen, Warren Buffett and Donald Trump are all not Jewish. Neither are the Saudi princes or the Mexican billionaire who purchased the New York Times. Despite absolutely looking Jewish to people who have never seen a Jew, Michael Jordan, LeBron James and Tiger Woods are not Jewish. The Pope wears a Yarmulke but is definitely not Jewish.

The 1970s television show *All in the Family* had Archie Bunker insist that Jews changed their last names so they could fit in. He cited "Morris Smith" and "Izzy Watson." At this point his son-in-law mentioned President "Abraham Lincoln," leading Archie's daffy but endearing wife Edith to exclaim, "I didn't know Lincoln was Jewish."[100]

At some point I may have to conclude that there are no rich Jews anywhere. The conspiracy nuts may then claim that the people who controlled everything used to be Jewish. My response would be that whichever non-Jews stole our money should give it back! I could ask if the people who stole it were Palestinians, but that would open up old wounds supposedly dealt with in prior chapters.

Another train of what passes for thought is that while many public billionaires are not Jewish, the people secretly controlling them are Jewish. So who are these people? Where does one find them?

Apparently it all comes down to the Federal Reserve. Central Bankers Alan Greenspan, Ben Bernanke and now Janet Yellen are all Jewish. Greenspan and Bernanke were both bald. Perhaps it is an outrage that Yellen was hired instead of a non-descript cue ball with a Jewish-sounding name. This could be a conspiracy of the follicly challenged, which would again bring us back to Corzine, Paulson, Trump, Pope Francis and Jordan. Jordan may be the most powerful of all of them. He started out as a basketball player. Now he owns an NBA franchise. He even has an entire Middle East country named after him.

If Greenspan and Bernanke were so powerful, how could they have been replaced? Bernanke was fired. Jews supposedly control the media. Couldn't the most powerful man in the world at the Fed have his friends in the media spin the story and save his job? Nazis carrying pitchforks did not do in Bernanke. College kids worshipping some non-Jewish octogenarian gynecologist demanded that the Fed be audited and abolished. The Fed survived but Bernanke was ousted.

I have heard that Jews control the Internet, but if we did we would hopefully be smart enough to ban anti-Semitic websites.

If a Jewish conspiracy existed, we would be the 99.8% and not the .2%. We would certainly own more land. At the very least we would have oil. We are the most powerful people in the world who control everything but we cannot even get a decent gusher of petroleum or natural gas. Maybe the conspiracy is so powerful that we have fooled people into thinking we control nothing. If that is the case, can somebody let my friends and me in on the joke and transfer a few billion dollars into our bank accounts? This whole financial struggle thing is irksome.

If there is no conspiracy, perhaps one day there will be no conspiracy theorists. Until then, the conspiracy nuts are so crazy that they make the anti-conspiracy nuts just as crazy with their craziness. I myself on occasion have been guilty of jumping to inaccurate conclusions.

As a child, I was convinced Santa Claus was an anti-Semite. He always skipped Jewish houses and only gave Christian kids presents. He was a jelly-belly Jew-hater. When I was eight years old I tried to sue Santa. I was too young to know what a class action lawsuit was, but I figured if Jews worldwide joined me we could take Santa down. Maybe we could use the settlement money to help spread Judaism and teach Christian kids not to accept gifts from an ethnic bigot. My father's exact words were, "Son, we need to talk." Ever since then, Santa has been good with me. He still does not give any of my Jewish friends or me presents, but in all fairness we never gave him anything either.

As a young adult I was not thrilled when my buddy J.J. bought a BMW. For one thing, I hate acronyms. For another, German efficiency is not reassuring to me. I do not blame the youth of today for what happened decades ago. One of my favorite rock bands of all time is German. With automobiles, it just hits too close to home given my family background. I told J.J. I did not want to ride in his car because, "My cousin Shlomo could be in the dashboard."

J.J.'s problem was that he let facts get in the way of my point. "Eric, you don't have a cousin Shlomo."

While this is true, he could have existed hundreds of years ago. Maybe the reason I don't have one is because he is in the dashboard. J.J. kept showing me features of his car. One button warmed the seats of the car and the car owner. If this was an American invention I would have been fine with a toasty posterior. As an anti-conspiracy hunter caught up in my own conspiracies, I had other ideas.

"J.J., that feature only exists for Jewish customers. One day against your will that feature will not turn off. They are trying to burn you alive in your own car!"

J.J. considered my theory, if by considered one means treated it as the idiocy it was.

Some people cannot tell when I am kidding, so let's settle this once and for all. I was serious about suing Santa and not serious about J.J's car. While I would not buy a German car, I would not freak out if I had to drive my non-German car through Germantown, Maryland. I cannot speak for the whole town but the one sports bar I visited allowed Jews to watch football games.

My one visit to Israel gave me the chance to avenge the blood of my great-grandparents. A restaurant had something on the menu called an Arab salad. I wanted to order an Arab salad and brutally stab it with a plastic fork. I even planned to shape the lettuce into the image of Yasser Arafat with an olive as his nose. I really hate olives. Then I noticed the picture on the menu. There was no lettuce or olives. It was diced cucumbers, tomatoes and onions with oil and vinegar. This seemed to be more of an Israeli salad than an Arab salad. First they try to steal our land and now they cannot even let us have our own salad! My girlfriend at the time shook her head as I asked the waitress what the difference was between an Arab salad and an Israeli salad. The answer was sickening.

"Nothing really. It is the same thing with a different name. Would you like one?"

I sulked and declined. After she walked away confused, I looked at my girlfriend and asked, "What's the point?" At least a Palestinian salad could have exploded in my mouth, but probably not from flavor. I know, I promised not to make those jokes. I get grouchy when reliving ruined dinners. I was a lousy justice avenger.

There was the time I got upset with somebody for recommending I turn on the local radio station to hear Hanukkah music. Instead the station was playing Christmas music. This seemed like an anti-Jewish conspiracy until I realized that two separate radio stations right next to each other on the F.M. dial could theoretically play two different songs. One had the Adam Sandler Hanukkah song.[101] The other station had a far more powerful radio signal. This is probably part of the anti-Jewish conspiracy. Otherwise the Christian station just paid more for a larger reach, proving again that the non-Jews had more of everything.

I could not understand why a sweet Catholic girl I liked when I was eleven years old decided to post a picture of herself on Facebook with an Adolf Hitler mustache. Thankfully I did not read her the riot act. On closer inspection it seemed that my computer had a strategically misplaced cookie crumb on it. I now wash my hands before using my computer. Otherwise eating spicy potato chips and then putting my fingerprints on the screen would leave red marks. Those marks could be mistaken for devil horns, which would inevitably be left on Jews. If anyone else becomes victimized by this problem, put the chips away and spray screen cleaner.

As for Nazis, why are they always so grouchy? They murdered us, yet they are the ones still complaining. What is the point of killing off two-thirds of a civilization if you cannot even take time out to enjoy it? Rest assured if Simon Wiesenthal had successfully hunted down every Nazi war criminal I would be smiling.

If Jews are so powerful, how come we cannot use our global network to find all the people who tried to murder us? Israel has not even tried to destroy France. We may be the only ones. Everybody else succeeded in crushing them. Between Germans and Islamists, France still takes marching orders from everybody except Jews. Nicholas Sarkozy was part Jewish, but so what? He was fired and replaced with someone who is…you guessed it…bald.

I just started a rumor that Zionist is an anagram for Stizoni (whatever that is). I will not rest until whack jobs decode the secret global Italian conspiracy. Sarkozy is married to Carla Bruni, who is Italian. Super Bowl champions win the Vince Lombardi Trophy, not the Jacob Greenberg Trophy. There is the plain Stizoni proof. Anagrams are more annoying than acronyms but less serious than angiograms. Oy vey, my heart can't take this topic anymore. It is all too crazy for me.

You may never encounter Zionist Crusader Alliance for World Domination leaders. We might be plotting stuff so secret that, like Jack Nicholson's Colonel Nathan R. Jessup said, "You can't handle the truth!"[102] Otherwise, we are busy hanging out, discussing politics, watching football, or taking a nap in the grand tradition of our Lethargy Club ancestors.

Chapter 17: Religious Lunacy: Not everyone is Jewish

I have been blessed as a Jew to live in New York and then Los Angeles. While Jews live in every corner of the world, this is often done quietly and with great discomfort. In big American cities, Jews are free to express their pride openly, loudly and proudly. This should never be taken for granted or seen as a given. Times change. Neighborhoods change. Many American areas have very few people and even fewer Jews. Being a Jew in these areas can be very isolating.

I would like to thank every rabbi, synagogue and Jewish dinner host who took a complete stranger traveling on business and made him feel like one of the locals. I also thank the many non-Jews across America who welcomed me into their homes and hearts. Many of these people know nothing about Judaism but respected my right to practice my traditions. My knowledge of their religions is also very low, but anything with one billion followers is serious business.

I have visited places with very few Jews but plenty of good people who love, honor and respect Jews. These are their stories.

Jews from South Florida to South Dakota

I remember my dad being surprised when I told him a couple of years ago that I met the Jews of Idaho. "I looked in the mirror. They were gorgeous."

I may have been. I hope I still am. Either way, there is Jewish life in Idaho. Chabad Rabbi Mendel Lifshitz is in Boise, along with other synagogues in Boise, Ketchum and Pocatello. Los Angeles and Manhattan Jews scoffing at the notion of Jewish Idaho would be mistaken for doing so. While Idaho's Jewish population is less than one-half of one percent, the world Jewish population is only one-fifth of one percent. Los Angeles and New York Jews are the statistical aberrations. Idaho is the norm.

Montana Jews have synagogues in Billings, Butte, Kalispell, and Missoula. Chabad Rabbi Chaim Bruk is in Butte. If one drives six hours West from Butte to Spokane, Washington, the approximate midpoint is Missoula. One can leave Butte on a Friday morning and make it to Spokane in time for Shabbos. There is even enough time on the way to stop by during the day and put on tefillin with Missoula Chabad Rabbi Berry Nash.

In a gorgeous area of rural Mississippi known as Pearl River, I asked a guy where I could find the local Jewish temple. He smiled and said, "New Orleans." The Big Easy in Louisiana was about 140 miles away. Was there anything closer? This proud redneck and proud Christian offered me wisdom and humor.

"Look, we have nothing against your people, but we can't force you to live here. We have every Christian church on the planet because every type of Christian lives here. Some of them have so many syllables in their religion that even they can't pronounce what they are. Jews are only one syllable but if you guys prefer Louisiana to Mississippi, that is where your temples will be built. We have great people, great music and great food. Y'all are welcome to come and welcome to stay anytime you want. Enjoy our Southern hospitality."

An old cliché is, "If you build it, they will come." A more modern idea is that they come first and then help build it. Jews are originalists. We do not wait. We act. We build stuff, even if we have to subcontract the actual construction work to non-Jewish day laborers. Jews have done enough hard labor throughout history. If the ability to subcontract exists, do it.

Some rabbis are Shluchim, emissaries of the Rebbe sent to spread Jewish life throughout the world. In Mississippi, Rabbi Akiva Hall was already there since his youth. Now he runs Chabad of Southern Mississippi. Biloxi,

Tupelo, Diamondhead, Hattiesburg and many other cities in Mississippi have synagogues of all denominations.[103]

In Natchez, Mississippi, Temple B'Nai Israel serves fewer than ten people. The synagogue has been donated to the Goldring/Woldenberg Institute of Southern Jewish Life. It must be preserved. This temple began in 1843 and peaked in 1907 with 145 members. The temple burned in 1903, and over 600 people attended the 1905 rededication ceremony.[104]

In one century the Jewish community dwindled. It may take another century to build it back up again. It may never be rebuilt, but one thing is clear. The weather in Natchez, Mississippi, is far better than the miserable conditions of New York. Those who enjoy intolerable muggy summer heat and winter blizzards may disagree.

What makes Jewish communities across the world special is the spice and flavor that occurs when local customs are mixed in with ancient traditions. Hawaii Jews greet visitors with a friendly "Shaloha." In Texas, it's "Shalom, y'all."

At Temple Emanu-El in Tucson, Arizona, Rodeo Shabbos is a big deal. When the rodeo is in town, these Southwestern Jews wear their big belt buckles and cowboy hats to temple. Adon Olam is sung to the tune of "Home on the Range."

While Nashville and Knoxville have thriving Jewish communities, the far Eastern part of Tennessee lacks a synagogue. The Tri-Cities area that includes Bristol brings in a rabbi from other parts of the country to lead holiday services. Bristol is a quiet area for fifty-one weeks out of the year. Then for one week about 100,000 people descend on the area for the annual NASCAR stock car race. A few years back Passover fell during race week. The rabbi declared it NASCAR Pesach and showed people the links between two great traditions. No, the late Dale "Intimidator" Earnhardt was not Jewish. Neither is Junior. However, NASCAR is a religion in the South. If Christians can celebrate two religions not in direct conflict, so can Jews. Moses lacked a car, but he and his followers sure moved fast when they had to do so.

Rabbi Jonathan Klein used to be at Hillel at the University of Southern California. I met him in the days right after the September 11 attacks. If ever there was a time to seek comfort in religion, that was it. Rabbi Klein made Judaism fun and relaxed without sacrificing its essence. His guitar version of Adon Olam was sung to grunge band Nirvana's, "Smells Like Teen Spirit."[105]

He performed this infrequently to protect the vocal cords he needed to give his Friday night sermons.

Preserving Judaism requires Jews of all religious levels to learn who and what they are. One mistake many Jews make is obsessing about other religions at the expense of Judaism. This is done for the sake of some perverse form of open-mindedness. At the UJ, one very good professor named Steve Lowenstein showed the students a flaw in this thinking. He asked us who Jesus's mother was. We knew the answer was Mary. Then he asked the classroom who Moses's mother was. There was stone silence. We had no idea. Her name is Jochebed.[106] I learned this about ten seconds ago. I just looked it up after writing the previous sentence. Professor Lowenstein may have told us the answer twenty-five years ago, but I do not remember either way. A couple of pretty girls in class distracted me by doing nothing but existing and breathing. Perhaps a mechitza is needed in classrooms as well.

Jews need to learn Judaism. There is only so much time to consume so much knowledge. The best and brightest retain more information, but even that reaches a cap. My childhood wall poster read, "Unlike stupidity, genius has its limits." I do not need extensive classes in other religions to learn the bare minimum. There are plenty of ways to gather information when it is absolutely necessary. Some lovely Christians taught me that in a beautiful way.

Several years ago a political women's group in rural Alabama invited me to speak at their Christmas party. The lady putting on the luncheon asked me over the telephone if I was comfortable calling their event a Christmas party instead of a holiday party. They really did not want to change the name. Their entire neighborhood was Christian. In that case, of course they should call it a Christmas party. They have every right to celebrate their traditions as they see fit. My Jewish friends in Los Angeles celebrated Hanukkah parties, not holiday parties.

Since Hanukkah that year fell during the Christmas party, she even suggested that I bring something Jewish to show everybody. I told her I could bring a menorah and light Hanukkah candles at the party. The group loved seeing the ritual performed.

The ladies were all served plates with ham. The waiter totally surprised me by bringing me a turkey plate instead. One of the ladies asked if she could get a turkey plate as well. The lady in charge said, "No, that is the only turkey plate. We made it special for him."

The other lady was understandably confused. A Christian woman in a Christian neighborhood who may have never met a Jew in her life should not be faulted for not knowing Jewish customs.

"Does he not like ham?" The group leader put an end to the discussion. "He is Jewish. He can't eat ham."

After the event was over, I had a chance to talk to the woman who put a ton of effort into making sure all of her guests including me were comfortable. "Thank you for the turkey plate. It was delicious, but I have a question. You said there were no Jews in this town. How did you know about the Jewish prohibition against eating pork products?"

She was honest and heartwarming. "The truth is we don't know much about y'all, but we wanted you to feel welcome. A couple of days before the event I went online and went straight to *Wikipedia*. I typed in the word Jewish and took it from there."

This is how people love thy neighbor. Her action was more than sufficient, or as we Jews say on Pesach, "Dayenu." We Jews should try to constantly learn and grow in our own faith. As for other religions, learning the basics is usually also Dayenu.

There are sadly far too many Jews with an unhealthy and irrational fear of Christianity and its worshippers. Most Christians are staunch supporters of Israel with a deep respect and in many cases love for Jews. When it comes to these Christians, secular Jews have a conspiracy theory that would make them right at home with those fearing the Illuminati. The theory is that evangelical Christians are only pretending to like Jews. The Christians want all Jews to move to Israel. Then the rapture can come and the Jews will all be replaced with Christians.

Any religion of one billion people will contain a few crazies. If 99.9% of all Christians are normal, that still leaves one million zealots trying to spread their crackpot theories around the world. Jews are the first people to accurately point out that it is unfair to blame one billion Muslims for the September 11 attacks. How can anyone with an ounce of intellectual honesty subject Christians to a different standard?

The only time anyone ever tried to aggressively convert me was in Salt Lake City, Utah. A few young missionaries chased me and caught up to me. They kept trying to hand me leaflets and insisting they were the one true faith. They would not leave me alone until I promised to consider their way of life.

When I told my friends that story, they wondered if the Mormons really were that relentless. Mormons? These were Libertarians demanding free marijuana and an end to the Federal Reserve.

The issue is not what other people believe, but whether they can enforce those beliefs and impose them on non-believers through coercion.

Rabbi Chaim Cunin taught me that Jewish law only applies to Jews. If he sees a Jew eating a bacon-cheeseburger, he offers the Jew an outstretched hand. He never shames the Jew. Over time he teaches the Jew the rituals of Judaism including the prohibition of pork. It is up to the person to decide to adhere to the rituals. If Rabbi Cunin sees a Christian eating a bacon-cheeseburger, he tells them to enjoy it. There is no religious violation since Christianity allows eating pork. Conversely, many Catholics believe they are not supposed to eat meat on Fridays. The staunchest Catholics would have zero objections to Jews eating meat at their Friday night Shabbos dinners.

If a Christian tells me that I will go to hell for not believing in Jesus, my response is a simple one. "No I won't. You're an idiot." Then the discussion ends because I choose to end it. Freedom of speech allows me to call out the idiocy of speech. It also grants my right to refuse to speak to those equating free speech with consequential speech.

Jews and Muslims have every right to ban pork products from synagogues and mosques. Those are their holy religious sanctuaries. Radical Islamists violate the live and let live principle. Some Muslim taxi drivers in Minneapolis, Minnesota and Dearborn, Michigan refused service to Christians with bacon-cheeseburgers and Jews with seeing-eye dogs. Forcing Jews and Christians to obey Muslim laws crosses the line. Moderate Muslims respect this distinction. Radical Muslims do not.

If a Christian puts a gun to my head or flies an airplane into the Towers, I may consider revising my views on Christianity. My faith is strong. I believe in my Judaism. I honor and respect the right of Christians to believe in the New Testament. They have to honor and respect my right to reject the New Testament for me. 99.9% of Christians respond, "Absolutely!" Where is the problem?

Another flaw in the secular Jewish attitude toward Christians is the assumption that all Christians are religious. Many Christians are secular. They just do not broadcast this worldwide like secular Jews do. There are plenty of Cafeteria Catholics. Many Christians go to church only on Christmas and Easter if at all. If you ask if they are still proud Christians, they say yes. This is no different than people living in ethnic neighborhoods. Most Irish and Italian people living in America are proud of their heritage. They are not subversives. They march in their annual parades and wax poetically about the old country but live here because they love being American.

There is a case to be made for Israel that has nothing to do with religion. The religious case for Israel matters to people who are religious. The secular case for Israel can be made to everybody. In the great tradition of Socrates and the Jews, questions must be asked. The first people to question are the secular Jews.

Ask secular Jews if they believe there is a moral equivalence between a dictatorship of Palestinians blowing up innocent civilians with suicide bombs and a democracy of Israelis trying to defend themselves. Most of them will concede these situations are entirely unequal. Now ask secular Jews if they think Christians are intellectually inferior. Are Christians the dumbest people on Earth? Are they too stupid to understand the simplest concepts that everyday ordinary people can grasp?

Most secular Jews do not think Christians are imbeciles. To feel that way would create an inconsistent line of concern. These Jews are afraid of Christians precisely because they see them as effectively nefarious. A person cannot be both evil and stupid. Those are contradictory traits.

Adolf Hitler was evil. Inspector Clouseau of *Pink Panther*[107] fame was an imbecile. They both had mustaches, which means nothing unless one runs the local mustache club. Those groups may teach that evolution is real because humans descended from walruses. No evidence exists that God had a mustache, although he could have had one if he wanted. Whether he could make his own schedule so busy that he would not have time to shave is a question for my grandfather in heaven.

For now, take the two questions and link them together. Secular Jews know the difference between a democracy engaging in self-defense and a dictatorship engaging in murder. If any person should understand this, and Christians are people, then connect the syllogism. Premise one plus premise two equals the conclusion that Christians have enough brainpower to handle this overwhelmingly simple idea. Maybe Christians support Israel because they just get it. After all, it is a pretty easy idea to get.

The secular case for Israel requires that Israel be treated no differently than Taiwan, South Korea or Singapore. All of of these nations are democracies within close proximity of non-democratic aggressors seeking to end their democratic way of life. In each case the enemy is a different enemy with a different religion. Standing up for democracies leads to a more peaceful world because there has never been a case in history where a legitimate democracy or republic attacked another one. As much as France bothers America, we settle our differences with sniping and snark rather than bombs and guns.

The only difference between Israel and the other democracies is that Israel is a Jewish state. If somebody lashes out at Israel while approving the exact same behavior by Singapore, then the issue is not policy. The critic is engaging in Jew-hatred using a fig leaf smaller than the ones that failed to keep Adam and Eve out of trouble. Similarly, any Jew who gives Muslims every benefit of the doubt while refusing to do so for Christians is being unfair. This is nothing but a fig leaf for anti-Christian bigotry by intolerant people engaging in misplaced projection.

Every Jew should just hug a Christian. Then watch how quickly and lovingly the Christian hugs them back. This is done out of honest goodness, not guile.

One last important lesson of religion is to not automatically believe everything you see and hear. Questioning things is acceptable. What they saw in my shul may have confused some Christian college students doing a term paper on various religions.

In the late 1990s, my friend Nate and I engaged in a ritual not sanctioned by any religion. At the Chabad House in Los Angeles, Nate and I would clink glasses and announce that the ceremonial exchanging of the neckties was about to begin. Nate's then-fiancée and now wife would just shake her head. Nate and I would remove our neckties and put on the other person's tie. This led to some dreadful color clashes. The next day at lunch we would announce the switching back of the neckties and trade them back.

It was harmless fun, but some people questioned whether this was codified Jewish law. The rabbi's five-year-old child wanted to partake. He wore a clip-on tie that barely reached my chest. To avoid my necktie dragging on the floor, I wrapped it around the child's head several times like it was tefillin. The next day we traded back. While I did not want to risk having my tie possibly get ruined, I also did not want the child to feel bad. Plus, the child was at a bigger risk by learning false customs. This kid was intelligent. I think he just knew I had a better necktie.

Luckily the non-Jewish college students were perceptive. They also quickly realized that the ritual where the rabbi's sons get a running start and cannonball themselves into the oversized trash bins is not part of halachah. Getting clean and nicely dressed up and then ruining clothing and getting filthy is normal to children of all stripes. It is a horror to those parents of all stripes. It is also amusing to outsiders of all stripes who understand that the greatest sound in this world is children laughing. This belief unites Jews and non-Jews from Southern California to South Dakota to South Florida to South Korea.

Chapter 18: Chai, how are you doing? Next Generation Lunacy

Another cliché is that those who do not learn from history are destined to repeat it. That was the threat high school teachers used to get kids to study. The only thing worse than flunking is summer school. Nobody can learn all of history but avoiding summer school requires learning between sixty-five to seventy percent of it.

A more important approach is to say that traditions die if they are not passed on through the generations. My father and his parents escaped the Nazis to save their lives. They made sure I knew that the reason their lives were ever in peril is because evil people wanted to end 6,000 years of Jewish traditions. I need to do my part to help Judaism survive for the next 6,000 years. Otherwise my family's survival and my very existence would have been in vain.

When I was in college, the next generation was merely a concept. Now it is a reality. My close friend and his wife adopted a child from Guatemala. Although this child has a real first name, his dad and I affectionately refer to him as "The boy." He is being raised Jewish. Long after his father and I are gone, the boy will be the next link in the Jewish history chain. His parents are handling the hard stuff like feeding, clothing, sheltering, protecting and raising him. I teach him the fun stuff.

Teaching the boy: Life lessons from Unca Eric

My friends met the boy when he was three months old and brought him back to the United States for good shortly after he turned one year of age in 2008. He has full citizenship and a letter signed by the president to prove it.

The adoption was mired in bureaucracy when Guatemala started toughening their adoption rules. My friends got in just under the wire, but it was still touch-and-go for a few weeks. In Thanksgiving of 2007, Jewish United States Senator Norm Coleman took a trip to Guatemala and helped solve the problem.[108] Most people think of politics as fights over abortion and gay rights. To my friends, Guatemalan adoption was a major issue. Thank God Senator Coleman felt the same way. He advocated on behalf of several families. Thanks to him, my friends brought the boy home. That is what makes the world a better place. That is the purpose of politics, lest people forget. The best word to describe Norm Coleman is *menschkite*.

As for the boy, my other nickname for him is "perspective" because he gives it to me whenever mine starts disappearing. When his father and I are watching the news and worrying about global terrorism, the boy comes over with his global agenda.

"Unca Eric, wanna play trains?"

Why yes, young boy, your Uncle Eric would absolutely like to play trains with you.

The more I look at the boy, the more he reminds me of a politician. Both the boy and politicians are adorable little gasbags. They both spend hours looking at and admiring themselves in the mirror. They should both work for the 3M Company because their favorite words are me, mine, and more. When they don't get their way, they both throw temper tantrums and need to be sent to their rooms for a timeout.

The late actor Art Carney offered a tradition that I have passed on to the boy, who has in turn passed it on to his friends. As Ralph Kramden's sidekick Ed Norton in *The Honeymooners*, Carney taught Americans an important sports ritual. When playing golf or baseball, the first thing a player has to do is address the ball. When the boy and his friends play, they start out by waving at the ball in a friendly manner and saying, "Hello, ball."[109]

The most important lessons the boy needs to learn are Jewish. His dad covers almost everything. I just fill in the gaps.

His first Jewish lesson came from *Star Wars*.[110] The boy likes to play with lightsabers. We duel. He always wins because he has the force, whatever that is. He is learning about geography and now knows that children play *Star Wars* lightsabers all over the world.

"Kiddo, do you know how they play *Star Wars* lightsabers in France?"

I taught him how and then he called his parents into the room. "Ok, show your parents how they play *Star Wars* lightsabers in France."

The boy dropped the lightsaber, fell to his knees, and said, "I surrender."

He brings tears to my eyes and melts my heart when he does stuff like that.

He loves helping his mom light candles for what he calls "Bat," also known as Shabbat. Hanukkah candles are extra fun because of all the different colors. He is too young to learn about the military blood triumph. For now, eight days of oil is what he is being taught.

At seven years of age he has already developed the skills necessary to become a successful capitalist merchant. He won a chess tournament for six-year-olds. Then he asked his mother to go on Facebook and find out if anyone knew how to go on eBay and help him sell his trophy for twenty dollars. Any day now I look forward to sitting down with him and showing him the *Wall Street Journal*.

Most importantly, the boy has a streak of decency inside of him that is a combination of heredity and a terrific parental environment. He gives the best high-fives on the planet. When I leave his home, he runs outside for one more hug. He is learning values that will make him a good Jew and a good person.

His parents teach him responsibility. They provide the love and the discipline. His Jewish educators spread the message of the religion and Jewish history. His synagogue gives him a Jewish community. All I have to offer the boy is unconditional love and one of the several pairs of tefillin my rabbi grandfather bequeathed me. Between all of us, the boy will be a beacon that extends Judaism to every corner of the earth with the power and brightness of a *Star Wars* lightsaber.

When he is taught the heart and essence of what it means to be a Jew, he can teach this to others. This is how we spread Judaism. This is how we extend Jewish history and all its accompanying beauty and glory. This is how 6,000 years of Judaism, even for those who missed the first 5,960 years or more, can be extended until forever.

Concluding Benediction

One purpose of a conclusion is for writers to sneak in stuff they should have included in the book but forgot. Then I guess I can wrap up with poignant endearing stuff.

I wanted to quote the song "Gesher Tsar Me'od"[111] because I like singing "lo lefached klal" very loudly. The world is a very narrow bridge.

If any of you know any single Jewish brunettes, I would be happy to give the girl's father or eldest living male kin a burnt offering of goats and lambs in exchange for her dowry. If the dowry is substantial I will even throw in Dijon mustard instead of regular mustard.

Here are some some gratuitous political remarks. I am absolutely against gay couples having abortions. I also think we should ban metrosexual marriage. Metrosexuals are beta-males. The Maccabees were alpha males. We need more tough alpha Jewish children.

I now think I know why so many synagogues have the word Adat in their name. According to my friend Jerry, Adat means congregation. Jerry is a director at a synagogue with the word Adat in it, so he could have made that up for no reason.

Now for the poignant endearing stuff.

If this book gets one more person to find happiness by leading a more Jewish life, it will have been worth writing. If this book gets me to find happiness by leading a more Jewish life, it will have been the best thing I have ever done.

I have a long way to go before the man I am and the man I need to become are able to converge. What I do know is that if the boy grows up to be a proud Jew, I will have played a tiny role in getting the biggest thing right.

I missed most of the first 6,000 years of Jewish history. I hope and pray that my love of being Jewish and ability to communicate that love will allow me to partake in the first few decades of the next 6,000 years. I wish that for all of you as well.

"*Yevarechecha Adonai veyishmerecha.* May God bless you and protect you. *Ya'er Adonai panav elecha veyichunecha.* May God's face give light to you and show you favor. *Yisa Adonai panav elecha veyasem lecha shalom.* May God's face be lifted toward you and bestow upon you peace."[112]

Hineni. Here I am. Jewish and proud of it always.

eric

Oh yeah, I forgot a few things. Cutting room floor lunacy

Music groups call it the B-Side. At concerts it is known as an encore. Judaism has the oneg after the service. We also have the Jewish goodbye after the actual goodbye. Shabbos and Yom Tov services have Musaf. For some people Musaf means more spirituality. For others it translates into an extra hour before the starving congregants get to eat. In the writing world, this extra stuff that is not quite a coda, epilogue or appendix is known technically as extra stuff. Extra stuff is slightly more prestigious than over-glorified navel gazing but fails to rise to the level of musings. Maybe it merited the cutting room floor. Discuss amongst yourselves while I take a nap and leave with you a prerecorded message about me.

When all is said and done, I might be the simplest guy on Earth. I can often be found with a soda and a burger, which is what I recommended to all of you before this adventure began. Actually, that was what I said in one of my other books. I meant to say it in this book but I forgot. Next time I will remember.

I laugh when my team wins, cuss for a few moments when they lose provided no children are in the room, and am lucky enough to have had the same friends my whole life. Watching football is about being with friends. I have the best friends a guy could ask for.

God created, loves and accepts me, flaws and all.

My favorite feeling in the world is when people who think they would not like each other meet and become lifelong friends. If that does not improve the world, I have no idea what does. So if you see me, no matter what your beliefs, approach me. Say hello. Offer a handshake or a hug.

Pull up a chair and tell me your story. It is the least I can do since I shared with you glimpses of mine.

As for me, my battle cry remains the same.

Hineni. Here I am. Jewish and proud of it.

So what next?

I'll be flying down the highway headed West…

In a streak of black lightning, called *The Tygrrrr Express*.

On to the next adventure. Shalom.

eric

Acknowledgements

My grandparents are gone, but with me always. My parents were never wealthy, but I was raised right.

Without love, there is no life. To previous romantic administrations, thank you for your love. My future romantic administration will be blessed because I learned from you. When you thought I was not listening, I was. I did care.

My friendships are lifelong friendships. They are listed in alphabetical order by last name to avoid any possible (insert nightmare scenarios here).

Seth Arkin, Brian Arnold, Richard Baehr, Michael and Ann Benayoun, Lin and Ed Bennett, Lara Berman, Johnny Ceng, Lisa and Bob Cohen, Nim Cohen, Chaim and Tova Cunin, Mendy and Rivkah Cunin, Seth Edelman, Brian Elfand, Jason Elman, Uri Filiba, Ken Flickstein, Deron Freatis, Eric and Jennifer Goldberg, Steve Goldberg, Cindy Graves, Eugene and Hilary Grayver, Molly and Leonard Grayver, Meredith Green Testa, Elyse and Aaron Greenberg, Larry Greenfield, Alan Greenstone, Danny Halperin, John Heller, Kevin Jackson, Julia and Marc Jaffe, Aryeh and Sharona Kaplan, Jason Kenniston, Tarik Khan, Jamie Krasnoo, Jerry and Jackie Krautman, Jeff Kuhns, Lisa Macizo, Mendy and Deenie Mangel, Jason and Lisa Margolies, Margie and Tom Mergen, Carl Merino, Mike Monatlik, Izzy Newman, Greg and Masha Neyman, Erica Nurnberg, Terry Okura, Mike Patton, Harold and Sharon Rosenthal, Jeanie Rosenthal, Ron Rothstain, Michael and Jennifer Rubinfeld, Daniel Savitt, Evan Sayet, Alan Schechter, Karen Siegemund, Alicia and Josh Stone, Brian Sussman, Ryan Szackas, Ruth and David Tobin, Dov and Runya Wagner, Grant Wallensky, Adam Wasserman, Armstrong Williams, Laura Wolfe, Nate and Janna Wyckoff, Sheri Yee, Oliver Young, Marc Zoolman. RIP Bernie Rosenthal and Borah Van Dormolen.

My extended family includes the Arzillos, Diels, Katzs, Mouradians, Rossis, and Weitzs. RIP David Malakoff and Janice Rossi.

Lara Berman convinced me to start a blog. Jamie Krasnoo provided the technological advice. Eliot Yamini of Hotweazel developed it.

Evan Sayet and Larry Greenfield helped me become a professional speaker.

Chabad rabbis are the best. God bless them all and the rebbetzins.

Long live the Zionist Crusader Alliance for never giving up the fight.

Almighty God, your patience with me is always appreciated.

eric aka *The Tygrrrr Express* http://www.tygrrrrexpress.com

Endnotes

(1) *Don't mess with the Zohan*, Debuted June 6, 2008

(2) Wright, Steven. *I have a pony*, 1985

(3) Bulwer-Lytton, Edward. *Richelieu; Or the conspiracy*, 1839

(4) *Ripley's Believe it or not*, Debuted March 1, 1949

(5) *Deal or no deal*, Debuted December 19, 2005

(6) *Miami Vice*, Debuted September 28, 1984

(7) *Dallas*, Debuted April 2, 1978

(8) *Torah, Book of Genesis*

(9) *Torah, Book of Leviticus, Pikuach Nefesh*

(10) Attempts to replace slogan with "Bed-Stuy and proud of it" in March, 2005

(11) History of the Jews in Southern Florida. *Wikipedia.org*

(12) Buchanan, Pat. *Wikipedia.org*

(13) *Torah, Book of Exodus*

(14) Ask the Expert: Kosher Symbols. *MyJewishLearning.com*

(15) Who knows one? Passover Haggadah

(16) Lederer, Edith M. U.N. says over 100,000 people killed in Syria. *Associated Press*, July 25, 2013

(17) History of Hamas. *Wikipedia.org*

(18) Duke, David. *Wikipedia.org*

(19) Seahawks blow out Cardinals in record fashion. *NFL.com*, December 9, 2012

(20) Refugee. *Wikipedia.org*

(21) Palestinian right of return. *Wikipedia.org*

(22) Arafat, Yasser. *Biography.com*

(23) Ibid

(24) Black September in Jordan. *Wikipedia.org*, Disputed claim of Yasser Arafat, September, 1970

(25) Fiallo, Fabio Rafael. Ariel Sharon's Masterstroke: The Gaza Withdrawal. *RealClearWorld.com*, January, 12, 2014

(26) 2000 Camp David Summit. *Wikipedia.org*

(27) Muslims in Miami Scream: 'We Are Hamas'. *Breitbart.com*, July 23, 2014

(28) *U.S. Department of State Office of the Historian*

(29) Arafat Horrified by Attacks, but Palestinians Celebrate; Rest of World Outraged. *Fox News*, September 12, 2001

(30) Many Palestinians rejoiced and saw space shuttle Columbia tragedy as divine punishment of Israel and America. *FactsofIsrael.com*, February 4, 2003

(31) Palestinians call for 'Day of Rage' against Israel. *Jerusalem Post*, November 7, 2014

(32) Hamas Caught Using Human Shields in Gaza. *IDFblog.com*, July 8, 2014

(33) Reform Judaism. *Wikipedia.org*

(34) Conservative Judaism. *Wikipedia.org*

(35) Golin, Paul. Just How Big is Intermarriage? You Don't Really Know. *TheJewishWeek.com*, August 14, 2014

(36) In National Survey, OU Finds That Orthodox Jewish Marriages Are Stronger Than In Society as a Whole. *Orthodox Union*, January 13, 2010

(37) *Torah, Book of Leviticus, Niddah*

(38) Rebbe Maharash. Lechatchilah Ariber, *Chabad.org*

(39) Opcit, 37

(40) Orthodox Inside Jokes: Mixed Dancing Makes Babies. *CrazyJewishConvert.Blogspot.com*, September 8, 2011

(41) Nesenoff, David. Looking over the Mechitza. *Chabad.org*, September 10, 2013

(42) Markoe, Lauren. 'Kosher Lust': Rabbi Shmuley Boteach says it's more important than love. *Religion News Service*, May 14, 2014

(43) *JDate.com*, December 24, 2014

(44) Davis, Al. *Wikipedia.org*

(45) Ibid

(46) Ibid

(47) Johnson, Billy. *Wikipedia.org*

(48) Temple Emanu-El, Birmingham, Alabama

(49) Maske, Mark. Ravens to play NFL's season-opening game on the road. *Washington Post*, March 22, 2013

(50) *NFL Primetime*, Debuted 1987

(51) Berman, Chris. *NFL Primetime*, Debuted 1987

(52) Ibid

(53) John Madden Football. *Wikipedia.org*, Debuted June 1, 1988

(54) *Mrs. Doubtfire*, Debuted November 24, 1992

(55) Smith, Will. Men in Black. *Big Willie Style*, Debuted June 16, 1997

(56) Sukkot and Simchat Torah. *Chabad.org*

(57) *Talmud*

(58) RaMbaM, *Mishneh Torah*

(59) Ferrell, Will. *Old School*, Debuted February 13, 2003

(60) Williams, Robin. *Late Show With David Letterman*, July 22, 2008

(61) Pfefferman, Naomi. Jon Voight, Chabadnik at heart. *Jewish Journal*, August 21, 2013

(62) The Rebbe's Last Message. *Inner.org*, February 13, 2014

(63) *SingaporeJews.com/history*

(64) *Traditionalmusic.co.uk*

(65) *AlanVeingrad.com*

(66) *AmericanThinker.com*

(67) Paraphrased from John "Woody" Woodrum, *San Diego Eagle Forum*, 2010

(68) Shurin, Dov. Madly in Love With the One Above. *Zochreini na*, Debuted 1999

(69) Jewish Population of the World. *JewishVirtualLibrary.org*

(70) *Little House on the Prairie*, Debuted September 11, 1974

(71) A Portrait of Jewish Americans. *PewForum.com*, October 1, 2013

(72) *Seinfeld*, Debuted July 5, 1989

(73) People of the Book. *Wikipedia.org*

(74) Affleck, Ben. *Boiler Room*, Debuted February 18, 2000

(75) *JesuswasnotaRepublican.org*

(76) *Torah, Book of Deuteronomy*

(77) Ethics of the Fathers: Mishnei Perkei Avot. *Shechem.org/Torah/Avot*

(78) Tzedakah. *Wikipedia.org*

(79) Ibid

(80) Caine, Michael. Alfred "the Butler" Pennyworth. *Batman: The Dark Knight*, Debuted July 16, 2008

(81) The Story of Hanukkah. *Chabad.org*

(82) Warsaw Ghetto Uprising. *HolocaustSurvivors.org*

(83) Six-Day War. *Wikipedia.org*

(84) Opcit, 25

(85) Rogers, Kenny. The Gambler. *The Gambler*, 1978

(86) *Ariel-Sharon-Life-Story.com*

(87) Bee Gees. Staying Alive. *Saturday Night Fever*, Debuted December 13, 1977

(88) *Dynasty*, Debuted January 12, 1981

(89) *Lifestyles of the rich and famous*, Debuted March 31, 1984

(90) Rock and Roll and the Fall of Communism. *Wikipedia.org*

(91) Krauthammer, Charles. Moral Clarity in Gaza. *Washington Post*, July 17, 2014

(92) Opcit, 81

(93) Libel: Israel murders and poisons. *Palwatch.org*

(94) Maghen, Ze'ev. Eradicating the 'Little Satan.' *Wall Street Journal*, January 5, 2009

(95) Stallone, Sylvester. *The Expendables 2*, Debuted August 17, 2012

(96) Krauthammer, Charles. *O'Reilly Factor*, 2012

(97) New World Order Conspiracy Theory. *Wikipedia.org*

(98) Ibid

(99) Flat Tire Cultists End up Deflated. *Associated Press*, December 29, 1992

(100) Stapleton, Jean as Edith Bunker. *All in the Family*, Debuted January 12, 1971

(101) Sandler, Adam. The Hanukkah Song. *Saturday Night Live*, December 3, 1994

(102) Nicholson, Jack as Colonel Nathan R. Jessup. *A Few Good Men*, Debuted December 11, 1992

(103) *Shluchim.org*

(104) *ISJL.org*

(105) Nirvana. Smells like teen spirit. *Nevermind*, September 10, 1991

(106) Jochebed. *Wikipedia.org*

(107) Sellers, Peter as Inspector Clouseau. *Pink Panther*, Debuted 1963

(108) Coleman optimistic about pending Guatemala adoptions. *Minneapolis Star Tribune*, November 24, 2007

(109) Carney, Art as Ed Norton. *The Honeymooners*, Debuted 1951

(110) *Star Wars*, Debuted May 25, 1977

(111) Gesher Tsar Me'od. *HebrewSongs.com*

(112) *Torah, Book of Numbers*

CPSIA information can be obtained
at www.ICGtesting.com
Printed in the USA
BVHW030943271018
530622BV00009B/2/P